Mighty Angels by Your Side

Tracey Howarth Tomlinson

2QT Limited (Publishing)

2QT Limited (Publishing)
Settle
North Yorkshire
BD24 9RH
United Kingdom

Cover and internal graphic images: shutterstock.com

Printed by IngramSparks UK Limited

A CIP catalogue record for this book is available
from the British Library

ISBN 978-1-912014-31-6

Acknowledgements

This book is dedicated to all the angels in my life, to my husband Mark, my sons Conor and Joshua, and to the numerous earth angels who have kept me sane and helped me on my path.

Get in Touch:
Website and blog: angelreis.com
Facebook: Tracey Howarth Tomlinson Author
Instagram: @tracey_rachel

Contents

Chapter 9

Chapter 10

Chapter 11

Chapter 12

Introduction

When I look back at my life, from where I once was to what I am now, I never would have thought I would have taken the path I have. Things have really accelerated for me since my spiritual awakening, when I truly opened up to the angels and their guidance.

In 2010 my life changed dramatically after attending an angel workshop. The angelic realm became a sense of wonder for me, there to assist and support me in my daily endeavours. There to help and guide me, my support network, my very own spiritual navigation system. Although there are many books on angels out there, I wanted to share their wisdom and guidance through the writing and compiling of this book. When I wrote my previous book *Walking into the Light* there were a few sections on working with angels. Originally that book started out as an angel book but then developed into something different. With this book I decided to go wholeheartedly with the subject of angels and share with you how, with their divine assistance, they can change your life for the better. Parts of the book will also look at where the names and ideas about angels came from.

Interest in angels has heightened in recent years. Stories of angels appear in magazines, in television reports and across all media. How people have been saved by angels, had visions of them, how angels have healed people or guided them in some way. Angels are everywhere. This interest has possibly come about from the search for a meaning to life as daily struggles take over, and from the stress that has resulted in the pursuit of material things. The angels give hope and inspiration in a frantic world and give faith that there is more to life than just the material things. When people start to question the significance of life they undoubtedly confront questions of a spiritual nature. They begin to enquire if there is more to life and seek out answers. The world of angels is a captivating subject to explore, and more and more of us are gradually opening up to the world of angels.

Angels are beings of light and are messengers of God, working on his behalf. Angels are powerful spiritual beings and there are many types of angel, which bring with them their own qualities and special virtues. Angels are there to assist humankind in their connection to God. Their role is to bring peace and God's will to those who open their hearts to angels. They can assist you in all areas of your life and give guidance and protection. All you need to do is ask. Angels cannot interfere with our free will choices. It is up to the individual to request help from angels, and these requests should be made with good intent and a sincere heart. Angels act on behalf of humanity to bring about peace to the world, and this is their divine mission.

In many stories of when angels appear their presence is always glorious and beautiful, and they are dazzling in their splendour. They are beings of light, radiant and exquisite to look at. General William Booth, the founder of the Salvation Army, had a vision of these angelic beings. He described them as having an aura of rainbow light that was so brilliant that it could not be looked upon by a human.

The term 'God' is used in this book, but for many people there are different words that they prefer to use, such as Creator, goddess, universal consciousness and so on. It's up to you, the reader, to use whatever terminology you find comfortable and to use your own interpretation of what God means to you.

In 2 Thessalonians 1:7 Paul speaks of the 'mighty angels of God'. Billy Graham, in his book *Angels*, likens the word 'mighty' to dynamite, that the angels are God's dynamite. In this book I wanted to give practical advice and share the techniques and knowledge that have helped me enormously over the years and that will also help you. When I have read books on angels I have asked questions, such as, 'Where did all these ideas on angels originate?' So I've put in some very basic information from the Bible and from belief systems that came from centuries past to give some idea about how our present-day understanding of angels has developed. As with any of my books, use what works best for you. Nothing is set in stone. If something does not resonate fully with you, that's fine. What works for some does not necessarily work for everyone.

Angels are found in many religious and ancient texts, dating right back to the ancient Sumerian culture. Whatever your religion or belief system I hope that you will find some things within these pages that are of use and can assist you. Biblical passages are used to show how angels appear in scripture and apocryphal texts (put simply, not included in canonical writings). I have put in ideas from texts to help you understand the nature and appearance of angels not as an academic understanding but to give an overview, an insight.

When working with the angelic realm, work with a sincere heart. No matter what your religion or belief system or how you live your life you can converse with the angels and bring them, their wisdom and their guidance into your being. They can help in so many ways with loving guidance, rather like a dear old friend who wants the best for us. They are there to be of benefit, to assist in all areas of your life, to steer you on your life's path and to guide you in a loving and positive manner.

Some of the foundations of angelology will be covered. Angelology focuses on the study of angels in religious texts. There are references from the Bible that are there to help us understand how the role of angels and their origin and existence developed, and how early Christian thinkers categorised the angels and assigned roles to them. There is also a reference section at the back, listing passages that can be found in biblical texts that mention angels. This section also contains any other references used in this book.

14

The Book of Ezekiel, however, is worthy of reading independently as it contains detailed information on angels at a deeper level. For this reason passages in Ezekiel are not noted in the reference section.

Use only the angel helpers and the tasks within this book with divine love. If you use anything in a negative way it will come back to you threefold. That is the way of karma. Use only what comes through on a loving vibration and with a sincere heart.

Reading about angels will help them be there by your side. Whenever anyone connects with the angels, they will be there rapidly by your side. They are there for everyone, even the most sceptical. They are there for every person regardless of their ethnicity, religious belief or sex. They are there regardless of behaviour, whether it is considered good or bad, and they are there for those who are in jail or who have performed good or bad deeds. Every human being has a guardian angel by their side. The angelic realm can assist in turning your life around, and can help in getting rid of addictions and in turning bad into good. All you need to do is to be receptive to their angelic presence.

In the process of writing this book I have been amazed at how information has come to me as if guided by an unseen hand. The angels want their message out there and in doing so have consistently and gently 'pushed' me to complete the book. At the time that I was writing this passage I received the news that I was to have a windfall of £500. I had been wondering how I was going to get my book published.

I had bills to pay and holiday expenses coming up, but knew that this work was to be completed and that the money would follow. And it has. When things are right, when you align to your true divine nature or higher self, synchronicities in life appear as if by magic, guided by unseen hands. They can help you too, putting things, people or opportunities on your path to assist you in your life's journey. It may not always be through windfalls of money. But be safe in the knowledge that if they can help you in whatever way possible they will.

Since I 'rediscovered' my angels back in 2010 I have devoured all number of books about them. I have angel oracle cards, angel pictures, statues and crystals carved in the shape of angels. My life is filled with angels. They are a constant reminder for me so I don't forget that they are there.

I hope you get as much from this book as I have from writing it. It has been a sheer joy, never a chore.

When working through the text, have a journal for recording any thoughts, dreams, impressions or events that occur so that you can revisit it in the future and measure how far you have progressed. Journals are a wonderful way of recording your spiritual journey and to look back on in the future.

In the appendices at the back you will find various meditations and prayers.

We live in a wonderful age, where information and communication can be instantaneously accessed at the touch of a button. There is so much more about the world than that we can touch, see, hear, taste or smell. There exists a realm beyond our natural senses, a realm that holds such wonder, divinity and grace, combined with unconditional love without judgement or prejudice. This is the world where angels reside.

Chapter 1

Why Angels?

Images of angels are found everywhere. From stained-glass windows, angel statues and ornaments, angel pictures and angelic jewellery, right through to shrines dedicated to the angels, such as Mont-Saint-Michel in Normandy, France to St Michael's Mount in Cornwall, England. Angels are everywhere.

There are even books on angels like this one. So why angels?

Something somewhere in your life will have drawn you to this book. Maybe it was the challenges in life. Maybe you are seeking an answer to your life's purpose, or are even questioning why you are here and what you are meant to do. Perhaps it was a tragedy that has prompted you to question life. Or maybe you have been inspired by other like-minded souls or preachers in your place of worship.

Connecting with the angelic realm may help you find the answers to these questions, but ultimately the answers reside within you. Angels may be the key to unlocking these answers and guiding you to a new path in life's great journey.

In my first book, *Walking into the Light*, I included various sections on angels and how they have assisted me in my life. For this book I want to focus more fully on the angelic kingdom and how angels can assist you in all areas of your life.

My belief system comes originally from my initial study of the Catholic faith. Although I had a belief in angels when I was younger, as I grew older I began to question that belief system, until eventually as an adult I left those beliefs behind. My angels were forgotten. It wasn't until many years later that I began to believe in angels once more. It was a pivotal moment in my life, one that changed my life forever and firmly set me on the spiritual path.

The catechism of the Catholic Church teaches us that, 'The existence of the spiritual, non-corporeal beings that Sacred Scripture usually calls "angels" is a truth of faith. The witness of Scripture is as clear as the unanimity of Tradition.' (Pope John Paul II, (2000).) *The Catechism of the Catholic Church* is a book written by Pope John Paul II that sums up the Catholic belief system. Of course, you don't need to be Catholic or have any sort of faith to believe. Belief in angels is not bound by religious systems or doctrines.

The angels are messengers of God. There are many different hierarchies of angels, and hundreds (if not thousands) of angels.

The Bible tells us that angels were created by

God the same as men, and that angels are invisible beings. The Bible also makes it clear that angels are non-material beings. Although they do not possess a physical body there are many reported instances where angels are believed to have appeared as men or women, and this is also evident in the biblical texts. Hebrews 13:2 points to how angels can appear in human form: 'Be not forgetful to entertain strangers: for thereby some have entertained angels unawares.'

The angels are found throughout the Old and the New Testaments. Some scholars believe that there are many angels (possibly in the millions). This idea comes from Hebrews 12:22, which speaks of a myriad of angels, and from Revelation 5:11–12, which speaks of angels by the thousands upon thousands and ten thousand by ten thousand. The number of angels that came down on Mount Sinai as God gave the law to Moses was ten thousand (Deuteronomy 33:2). These passages in the Bible indicate that there may be a multitude if not thousands of angels working in the heavens. In Revelation (10:1) the angels descend from heaven, having immeasurable brilliance, face shining like the sun, feet as pillars of fire. This is similar to Daniel (10:6), where the angel's face has the appearance of lightning, eyes as lamps of fire and feet like polished brass.

Scholars have also established a hierarchical order of angels, in which guardian angels and archangels are classified (this is discussed in a later chapter). These ideas stemmed from clues in biblical texts.

When I began working with the angelic realm I

found it simpler to work with the major archangels. The archangels are high-ranking angels. They can be found in many religious texts, particularly those from Judaism, Christianity and Islam. You can call upon angels for assistance at any time. You will not be taking them away from essential tasks, as they can be in many places at once.

Each angel brings with them a special virtue or quality. They are the connections of humans to the divine consciousness, or God. Their role in life is to bring peace and God's will to those who open their hearts to the angels. They cannot, however, interfere with one's free will choices.

It is up to the individual to ask for the help of the angels. These requests must be made from the heart and of good intent, so don't ask them for the lottery numbers. They will, however, help guide and protect you in positive ways.

My deep connection with the angels came in 2010, when I attended an angel workshop facilitated by my friend Julie. That time was a very low point in my life. I had gone through marital difficulties, and although my husband and I were back together the aftermath of it had brought my energies down.

I really connected with the angelic realm that day, and since then have been inspired and guided by the angels. My entire perspective of life changed that day. Connecting with the angels lifted me in ways I never thought possible. I still occasionally face problems in life, as we all do at some point, but knowing I have the angels on my side means I always have the strength and energy to tackle those issues. I was guided to use the angels in healing and subsequently trained in Angelic Usui Reiki, guided by the angelically inspired Yvonne. My life has improved greatly through connecting with and being guided by the angels. As I am writing this I feel the angel connection coming through. It gives me peace and a sense of loving wisdom.

We all have free will, and so the angels cannot assist us unless we actively request them to do so. This is because angels cannot interfere with our free will choices.

We can ask the angels for things that will be of benefit to our highest nature. We cannot, however, ask the angels to interfere with another person's free will. It just doesn't work like that. We can, though, ask for things that make our lives happy and peaceful, for things that are for the good of ourselves and of others.

Angels cannot be summoned to do anything that is not at one with good or God's light. Nor must we worship them, as they are purely God's helpers and messengers. Instead we give all the glory to God, the divine, or whatever name you identify with most closely. Angels act on God's behalf by bringing peace to the world, and this is their divine mission. When we live our life in a more peaceful way we are more in tune with our authentic self.

My angels are always with me, as your angels are with you. Sometimes I get caught up in daily life and I 'forget' about them. Then when I 'remember' them

I consciously connect with my angels and they are there by my side.

During more recent years, with the increase on the focus on material wealth, troubles in the world and personal challenges, people have begun to turn their attention to more spiritual matters. They are turning their attention to the significance of life and are facing questions of a more spiritual nature. Is there more to life than this and, if so, what? Angels bring a certain light into one's life. They bring hope and a belief that there are celestial beings available to assist in the challenges that confront us daily.

People are opening up to the presence of angels more than ever before. Angels are the messengers of God. They are here to help, heal and guide us. They exist on a higher spiritual plane and vibrate at a different frequency from ours. Some people find it easier to tap into this vibrational frequency than others, but we can all endeavour to raise our vibrations to commune with the angels.

Angels are God's messengers in that they take our messages, requests and problems directly to God. They are life's helpers and guides. Ultimately, all glory goes to God.

Angels and angelology were prevalent in the old belief systems and were written about by medieval scholars, such as Saint Bonaventure (1221–1274), Thomas Aquinas (c.1225–1274) and Pseudo-Dionysius, a Christian theologian and philosopher of the late fifth and early sixth centuries.

Angels continued to be written about in works by

Rudolf Steiner (25 or 27 February 1861–30 March 1925) in the late nineteenth and early twentieth century, and by popular authors in the present day like Doreen Virtue and Diana Cooper. There is a wealth of books, literature and thought through the ages about the existence of angels. Angels can assist you in every area of your life.

The work of Rudolf Steiner helped shift the view of angels from the religious to the more humanistic. A German scientist and philosopher, he developed a deep understanding of the angels. He believed that as we became more evolved as human beings the more connected to the angels we would become. Steiner suggested that angels work through images, and he suggested that we need to work on our intuition and imagination to decode these images. Steiner thought that angelic teaching had a threefold purpose. This was that each person would find their own link with divinity, that they would come to live in freedom, and that they would honour the divine source within themselves and others.

Angels are here to help, guide and protect us. Angels can help to bring peace to the world and ultimately to us, as individuals, one person at a time. If we live in a more peaceful way we become more in tune with our authentic self and we express ourselves with increased love in our hearts. To honour the peaceful, loving part of our self is to embrace our true nature and to step on to the path of peace, happiness and abundance.

When carrying out any of the exercises in the book,

or in connecting with the angels, keep a journal at hand to record any experiences or feelings you may have. Journaling will help record your development, and what you write can be kept for later reflection to see how far you have progressed.

What are Angels?

Angels are God's messengers sent down to Earth to give guidance and to raise the vibrations of the Earth and its inhabitants.

The angels are there to give guidance and hope, to spread the light of God and to elevate the vibrational levels of all sentient beings. They are full of God's love and they send our prayers back to God so that they may be fulfilled. They will never do harm, nor will they promise gifts of great wealth. They will, however, steer you in the right direction in life and give guidance.

When they are present they will feel light and airy and full of love and devotion. They will never feel angry or oppressive. They would never hold any person in judgement or condemnation. They are always there to give guidance and support and to uplift our spirits.

When guidance comes from the angels you may feel a thought being repeated in your mind or a continued sense of urgency to do something. The thoughts or ideas that come from angelic guidance would not feel ego-based.

For example, in writing this book I have felt a constant but gentle pressure to get it done to the exclusion of other, less important things. There has been a focus of energy put my way to encourage and guide me to write, to create and to spread the message of the angels. It is a message of hope, inspiration, peace, tranquillity and love. You yourself may find this when you connect with the angelic realm. It may come in the way of needing to change your diet to something healthier, to undertake volunteer work in the community, to train as a healer, to visit places associated with angels or to read divinely inspired books.

When I connected with the angelic realms and my mood and emotions automatically lifted, I felt such an overwhelming peace and an inner knowing that I could work through any problems with their assistance and guidance. I was guided to buy angel books, and books that would lift my spirits and inspire me. I was especially guided to start healing and was guided to exactly the right people who would help me on my path.

From there I went to ceremonies at various stone circles, including Stonehenge and Avebury. I met some wonderfully inspiring people who were on the same path as me, and I got to explore and open up spiritually in a way that I had never experienced before. It was, and still is, truly magical. That's what a deep connection with the angels can give you: a sense of magic and joy. When I first opened up to the angels I felt an excitement, an enthusiasm and an optimism that I had not felt for a long time. It was like being a child again: finding and discovering new things and feeling excited about the future once more.

The angels are constantly by my side, giving me guidance, support and encouragement. They elevate and uplift my spirits and give me happiness and hope.

They are like a spiritual satellite navigation system, steering me on my way to new and wonderful destinations, experiences and people.

Their love, support and angelic guidance have helped me write this book and the one before it. Their message is clear: align your being to the love and wisdom of God through their angelic guidance. To love and be loved. Love, the one universal truth, is all there is.

Experiences related to the acquisition of material things leave an emptiness within them. Once you acquire one thing you strive to replace it with something else. The happiness gained from that new car or home is fleeting. These things need to be maintained, updated and constantly improved. We might look at our possessions and find fault … this could be better, that could be improved … the neighbours have something better than us.

The angelic realm can guide us to explore new and different realities within ourselves that are not reflected by material wealth or possessions. That does not mean that it is bad to have such things. It means that we should not form attachments to such items, and not place value on the acquisition of stuff to fill the empty void in our souls.

Connecting to the divine source and being in a state of conscious allowing can and ultimately will fulfil us and satisfy our needs. It will fill the void, the empty space that can sometimes exist in our hearts and minds.

How Angels can Help

The angels are God's messengers. They are here to give us help, support and assistance while we are here on the earthly plane. The mission of the angels is to give our prayers directly to God, the Creator, the universal spirit, the universal consciousness, or whichever term feels comfortable to you. According to Billy Graham, 'The most important characteristic of angels is not that they have the power to exercise control over our lives, or that they are beautiful, but that they work on our behalf.' (Graham, 1994.)

There are many different hierarchies of angels and hundreds, thousands, or possibly an infinite number of angels ready to help in all aspects of our lives.

Each angel brings with them a special quality or virtue. They bring peace and love to those individuals who open their hearts to the angels. They cannot, however, interfere with our free will choices. They can only assist us if we ask them to do so.

The angelic guidance may come through patterns of thought. There may be a recurring thought that comes to you which encourages you to complete a given task. Perhaps something you have asked for may be placed on your path, or you may hear subtle voices speaking to you. Any influences that the angels put your way will be loving and peaceful and always positive in nature, never negative or harmful to you or others.

Some angelic communication may come as symbols or images. When I first began to work with guidance from the angels I began to receive symbols and sometimes images in my mind. I would wake up with symbols in my mind, which I would then research to find their meaning. Often I would receive images in my mind's eye. As I write this passage I feel a connection to the angels as a warm feeling across my back – a slight pressure, almost. Sometimes it comes as a gentle nudge or a pushing sensation.

I know that I am being pushed to write this book on angels, to spread their message of love and wisdom and to share their gifts with mankind. As I write I do not know what the title will be or indeed how it will be published. But I know that I have to write it and that I am being guided to do so, even though there are many books out there of a similar nature. I currently wake up each morning being pressed with a sense of urgency to write this book, and I know that the guidance I am receiving comes directly from the angelic realm. Know that there is a divine order in the universe, an intelligent consciousness that exists behind all creation, and the angelic realm is a part of it.

A question arises: Does God send angels to rescue people from every painful circumstance? The answer is no, as unfortunately pain and suffering are a part of the human existence and no one is immune. But in our darkest moments the angels can be there at our side, helping us to move through these experiences with their guidance and taking our prayers directly to God. These dark nights of the soul can be a chance to shine light on what has gone wrong in our life and how we can move through these experiences to ultimately develop a happier and more fulfilling life.

There are many stories, however, of people who believe that angelic beings have saved them from danger. This may be because it is not that individual's time to be a part of that particular experience or event. In other words, angels will intervene if the event is not part of that person's life plan to experience that particular, possibly life-threatening instance. I truly believe that we do not pass over to spirit or die before our time is due. And, as such, at that point angels will step in and assist to stop a catastrophe.

When we think of angels they will be there at our side. In fact they are always at our side, ready to assist. Everyone is assigned a guardian angel. Some believe we have two, assigned to be with us throughout our earthly existence. We can connect with angels through our hearts and minds.

To help us connect more clearly with angels we need to work on raising our vibrational frequency or, in other words, our auric vibration. This can be done by meditating regularly and connecting on a subconscious level to the divine realms. When we meditate it calms our mind and emotions and helps to alleviate stress.

As the mind slows down it shifts. You can tap into the levels of consciousness that exist outside our own physical existence. There are many layers of consciousness that exist, and one of those layers is where you can access angelic wisdom and guidance. During meditation the energy field that surrounds you will lift and become more expanded. When connecting with the angelic realm a subtle shift in energy may be experienced as the vibrational field surrounding the body becomes more expanded and less dense. This shift is all part of the experience and is not to be feared.

Your mind and thoughts are also a part of the divine source, the consciousness that is a part of the ever-flowing universe. You have free will, but you are also a part of the divine source, of God – the structure that holds the universe together. Begin the process of allowing spirit and the angels to work with you and through you. Align your intentions to the source of all that is and your life will come into spiritual alignment, away from ego.

When you shift your thoughts away from the spiritual towards ego you weaken the connection with the divine source or God. Your free will can either move in conjunction with the divine source and flow with it or it can move away from it, towards the dominance of the ego. As it moves away from the divine source towards ego your life will become more of a struggle, with feelings of hopelessness, of feeling helpless and lost – feelings that will permeate your being.

Use your free will to connect with the divine source and the angelic helpers, and allow your life's path to evolve without so much of a struggle or of feelings of despair. Know that the angelic realms are there to help you, to guide you and to protect you as they steer your path to spiritual illumination and enlightenment to be a part of God's divine source and plan. Begin the process of allowing angelic spirit to work with you, not against you.

Your angels are there to help with all aspects of your life. Regularly ask the angels for help and guidance with situations, however large or small. However, remember that angels cannot interfere with divine law, so you cannot use them to exert your will over others. There are some experiences that we must go through while we are here on the earthly plane. These are all part of our existence, but if the angels can help they will. If there is a difficult life experience that you must go through you can be safe in the knowledge that the angels will be there by your side to support and guide you to achieve the best outcome for you, according to God's divine plan.

Angelic Guidance

In writing a passage it never ceases to amaze me how I am directed to the right information that is required at that time. The angels absolutely guide me to the right books, the right passages of information, the right people. Just as I was writing then I wanted some information about an angel. My eye was immediately drawn to one of my books (I have rather a lot). On picking it up I was drawn to open it up on a particular page out of the four hundred pages to choose from.

Randomly (or maybe not) I opened the book on the exact page that told me about this specific angel, one of the Kabbalistic angels and not a particularly well-known one. As if by a miracle it was the information that I needed to know – revealed as if guided by some divine hand.

This has happened to me a lot over the years. If you ask for guidance from your angels, one way or another it will come to you.

My first book, *Walking into the Light*, took a number of years to complete due to the personal circumstances that diverted my energies into other areas of my life.

In the spring of 2017 I had a call from a self-publishing company in America who had got my details from a form I had completed online and had forgotten about. I had thought no more of it and so was surprised when they rang me out of the blue. After checking their credentials and reviews online I decided not to go with them. That call, however, did spur me on to write my book and to get it finished once and for all.

I cleared a slot over the summer and settled down to my writing. At many points during that time I really thought that my book was never going to be finished, but I ploughed on.

As if by magic, my writing all began to fall into place. Ideas and inspirations came to me as if placed there by divine guidance. I broke apart some of my original writing and put it back together in a new way, a bit like a jigsaw. New chapters flowed to me.

Eventually I was finished, two weeks later than

planned, but it was done. I felt that I was now at a point where I could look for a publisher.

I searched online for a publisher but there were so many I felt overwhelmed. I looked at the screen full of lots of publishers with anxiety developing in the pit of my stomach. I sat back, took a deep breath and shut my eyes. I asked for guidance from my angels. On opening my eyes there was one publisher in particular that jumped off the screen. Their office was in the next county, about an hour's drive away, so I arranged to meet the owner.

The drive was perfect, the weather was beautiful, the journey through the Lancashire and Yorkshire countryside was scenic and I found the place with such ease. When I got to their office everything just seemed to fit into place. It felt right. I believe I was directed there by the power of the angels.

My book was successfully published. There was a different meditation symbol placed at the beginning of each chapter, suggested and chosen by the editor. Even more amazing was that this had been predicted by a medium during a reading she had done for me four years earlier.

These are just some of the examples of how my connection to the angels has helped me. What I do now is listen to that inner guidance and work with it.

The archangels lead many other lesser angels in their work. They are all working in conjunction with God's will and for the benefit of humankind. For the beginner it is always best to work with the archangels initially, as I feel they are easier to commune with. As with all work with the spiritual realms, the energies you work with should be loving and positive. If it does not feel right ask them to leave. Always ask to work with beings of pure, loving light.

You may call upon the angels to assist with any situation at any time. You will not be taking them away from any other work, as they are omnipotent. This means that they can be in multiple locations at the same time.

You can request the angels to help with all sorts of situations in your everyday life. The most common problem areas in our life are our relationships, our careers, our family life and issues surrounding our finances. However, the angels cannot work against the free will of others. For example, you cannot use the angels to coerce other people against their free will, such as making them fall in love with you.

You can, however, ask the angels for help and guidance for the highest good of yourself and for others. The end result might not be what you expect. But it may be something even better, something that you hadn't even thought of.

The angels will hear your request and work their magic in divine and wondrous ways.

Chapter 2

The Seven Major Archangels

In this section we will look the major archangels. Although we associate each angel with a feminine or masculine aspect, angels really are neither. The terms 'his' or 'her' are used for each angel, but you can decide for yourself.

There are many angels and archangels named in various religious texts, and it is easy to become confused by them all. In popular literature about the angelic kingdom there are approximately fifteen archangels. However, for the purposes of this chapter we will look at the seven major archangels.

There are only two angels named in biblical texts: Michael and Gabriel. Raphael appears in the Book of Tobit, an apocryphal text. In the Book of Tobit (12:15) Raphael declares his true identity by revealing he is 'one of the seven angels who present the prayers of the saints' to God. A similar phrase is also found in Revelation 8:2, 6 (Keck, 1998).

Pseudo-Dionysius gives the major archangels as Michael, Gabriel, Raphael, Uriel, Chamuel, Jophiel and Zadkiel.

The names of the seven major archangels vary according to tradition but the names Michael, Gabriel, Raphael and Uriel are consistent within most traditions. Variations of the other three are Raguel, Zarachiel and Remiel.

Archangel Michael

His name means 'he who is like God'. He is the most powerful of all the archangels and is considered the leader of them. He is referred to as the prince of heavenly hosts.

Archangel Michael is in charge of a group of angels known as the order of the virtues. He inspires light workers to carry out healing, and tasks of a spiritual nature. In healing work he can assist in conjunction with Archangel Raphael.

Many places of worship are dedicated to Archangel Michael. When Salisbury Cathedral was constructed, between 1220 and 1258, altars were built in honour of him. Many chapels and buildings were built out of respect to Michael. Shrines in Monte Gargano and Mont-Saint-Michel were built to celebrate the specific appearances of Michael. He is considered the most important angel to call upon for the protection from evil and demonic entities (Keck, 1998).

September 29 each year is dedicated to the Feast of Saint Michael and All Angels. He is the patron saint of police officers, soldiers and firefighters. Traditionally he was believed to be the first of all archangels to be created.

Michael has played a role in human history, together with the saints. Joan of Arc (1412–31) received various visions from many saints, including Archangel Michael. He guided Joan of Arc when she led the French armies against the English in the Hundred Years War. Michael also appeared to three children in Fátima alongside the Virgin Mary in 1917. He appears in scripture and in many Jewish and Christian apocryphal texts and he taught Adam to farm in the Garden of Eden (Keck, 1998).

Michael is usually depicted as carrying a sword, which he uses to set us free of fear and to cut etheric cords of attachment. When he is present you may see flashes of purple or bright blue.

He can be called upon to guide you in your life's direction, purpose or career path. He can motivate and guide you on your path and help overcome addictions and increase self-esteem. He can be called on to fix mechanical and electrical devices. He is a strong defender of righteousness.

Michael is the angel of the Last Judgement, where he weighs the souls to establish their fate. He is the patron angel of justice, mercy and righteousness. He assists in situations where you may be confused, afraid or concerned for your safety.

Oversees:
- Element of fire
- Southern quarter of the Earth

- Autumn season
- Astrological signs of Aries, Leo and Sagittarius (Andrews, 1992).

In the Bible he appears in Daniel 10:13, 10:21 and 12:1, Jude 1:9 and in Revelation 12:7–9.

Keywords: addictions, career path, courage, cuts cords of attachment, healing and spiritual work, motivation, life direction, life's purpose, protection, wards off evil and lower entities.

Archangel Raphael

This angel's name means 'God heals'. He is the angel of physical and emotional healing, and a powerful healer of animals and people. Raphael can be called upon on behalf of others but, as with all angels, cannot interfere with a person's free will choices. He is the patron of all travellers and watches over them to ensure a safe and harmonious journey.

The Book of Tobit shows that Raphael and his colleagues could help deliver miraculous cures to those who needed them.

Raphael played a central role in the Book of Tobit as he assisted Tobias (Tobit's son) on his journey and kept him free from harm. The Book of Tobit is not part of the biblical canon in Protestantism. Tobias was shown by Raphael how to use fish parts in medicinal ways. As a result, Raphael guides healers to the correct treatments for ailments. Raphael also appears in the Book of Enoch. He is accredited with healing

Abraham of pain after his circumcision, which he underwent in old age.

Raphael is known as the patron of travellers, and he helps with all aspects of travel as well as spiritual journeys. Raphael is often depicted as bearing a staff. He specialises in healing, creativity, space clearing, spiritual release and clairvoyance. He pays special attention to those on religious pilgrimages or who are developing spiritually.

Archangels Raphael and Michael often work together in healing and also in guiding lower energies away from people and places. Raphael is credited as giving Solomon a ring engraved with a five-pointed star (a pentalpha), which had the power to defeat all demons.

His presence may be indicated by flashes of emerald green.

Having cured Tobit of his blindness, he is the patron saint of the blind. He can help us become a clear seer by helping clear our third eye to develop clear inner vision.

Oversees:

- Element of air
- Eastern quarter of the Earth
- Spring season
- Astrological signs of Gemini, Libra and Aquarius (Andrews, 1992).

As he is referred to as the archangel of healing, he also may be alluded to in John 5:2–4 in the Bible.

Keywords: animal healing, creativity, developing spiritually, eyesight (spiritual and physical), healing, physical and emotional healing, releasing lower entities, space clearing, travelling.

Archangel Gabriel

Gabriel's name means 'strength of God' or 'God is my strength'. She is God's holy messenger and was the angel that told Mary of the future birth of Jesus. She is traditionally venerated as the archangel of prophecy, revelation, mercy, wisdom and visions. Gabriel appears in many apocryphal Jewish and Christian sources.

Gabriel assists with the adoption or conception of children. She can help anyone whose life purpose involves art or communication, such as actors, singers, writers, teachers or dancers. Those who deliver spiritual messages can call on this angel to assist them.

Gabriel is the angel of positive action, and those who ask for assistance will be pushed towards a positive direction.

Gabriel is traditionally depicted carrying a lily (Mary's flower), a scroll and a sceptre.

Oversees:
* Element of water
* Western quarter of the Earth
* The season of winter
* Astrological signs of Cancer, Scorpio and Pisces (Andrews, 1992).

In the Bible Gabriel is found in Daniel 8:16, 17, Daniel 9:21, Luke 1:5, Luke 1:19 and Luke 1:26.

Keywords: adoption of children, conception of children, artists and media, communication, dreams and visions, mercy, positive action, prophecy, wisdom.

Archangel Uriel

Uriel's name means 'God is light'. In some traditions his name means 'fire of God'. Although Uriel cannot be found in canonical writings he is venerated as one of the major archangels. The Eastern Orthodox Church and the Anglican Church still venerate Uriel as an archangel.

Uriel appears in the Book of Enoch. He shines his light on situations or may give prophetic messages. He is the angel of wisdom and intelligence. He warned Noah of the Flood, assisted the prophet Ezra to predict the coming of the Messiah and gave the Kabbalah to mankind. He is also associated with alchemy.

In the Second Book of Enoch (also known as the Slavonic Book of Enoch) Uriel is replaced by Phanuel in two places in the same book (Ronner, 1993).

Through Uriel comes wisdom, the giving of practical solutions to problems and insight into creative endeavours. Uriel is associated with the elements of weather, such as thunder and lightning, and helps with earthquakes, floods, hurricanes, fires and other natural disasters.

Uriel is considered the angel of prophecy and interpretation and can be called upon to inspire writers and teachers. His symbols are traditionally the book and the scroll or an open hand holding a flame.

Uriel is considered as an interpreter due to his appearance in 2 Esdras, an apocryphal book of the Old Testament.

- Oversees:
- Element of earth
- Northern quarter of the Earth
- The summer season
- Astrological signs of Taurus, Virgo and Capricorn (Andrews, 1992).

Keywords: alchemy, creative projects, interpretation, natural disasters, practical solutions, prophecy, teachers, weather, wisdom, writers.

Archangel Chamuel

His name means 'one who sees God'. He is considered to be a peaceful healer of relationships. He is also considered a leader of the heavenly hierarchy known as the powers. As such, he protects the world from lower energies and protects us from those who wish to control the world in negative ways. He can also help protect our personal world. He can be called upon to help us find lost items that are physical as well as non-physical things, such as our life purpose, our relationships or our careers. He can help you find the things that you are seeking in your life, such as the right place to live, your soulmate or whatever you are seeking. Like Gabriel, Chamuel is the angel of Gethsemane and gave Jesus strength with the assurance of his resurrection.

Archangel Jophiel

This angel's name means 'beauty of God'. Traditionally known as the patron of artists, she was present in the Garden of Eden, where she was associated with guarding the tree of knowledge, and later with watching over Adam and Eve's three sons. Her symbol is traditionally the flaming sword. According to the Torah, she is a companion angel of Metatron. She helps us see the beauty around us and to think beautiful thoughts. She can also be called upon to beautify our words and deeds, and to generally beautify our lives. She helps with creative and artistic endeavours and can help beautify the spoken and written word. Calling upon her can help turn around unpleasant situations.

Archangel Zadkiel

This angel's name means 'the righteousness of God'. Zadkiel's symbol is traditionally the sacrificial knife, as some believe it was Zadkiel who stopped Abraham sacrificing his son to God (other sources suggest it was Archangel Michael). According to rabbinic writings he is the angel of mercy, memory and benevolence, and is in charge of the order of the dominions. He can help you feel mercy and compassion towards yourself and others. He helps facilitate forgiveness and helps us see the divine light in everyone. He can help with our remembering of our life's purpose. He can be called upon to assist in memorising information, or with assisting your memory in general.

Chapter 3

Other Archangels and Beings of Light

Archangel Ariel

This angel's name means 'lion or lioness of God'. This angel appears in the ancient Jewish Apocalypse of Ezra. When she is near you may experience visions of lions, and she is also associated with the wind. She oversees watery environments, as well as the protection and healing of nature. She helps with the protection of wild animals and works closely with Archangel Raphael to heal animals. You may sense a change or breeze in the air when she is with you. She can be called upon to assist in environmental matters when nature is in danger, such as developments on greenfield sites. She works closely with the fairy realm and the elemental realm. She can help manifest with earthly needs, such as help with finances.

Archangel Azrael

His name means 'God helps'. His aim is to assist

people at the time of their passing. He also helps people to cope with their grief. Azrael can be called upon to comfort those who are dying and to help with their crossing over. His energy is believed to be quiet, comforting and composed. He guides souls to the kingdom of heaven. Azrael will also help you find the answers to questions that you may have, and also to find trust and faith.

Archangel Haniel

Her name means 'glory of God'. She is associated with the moon and the planet Venus. The ancient Babylonians called upon her to assist in divination and healing work. She will help with clairvoyance and intuition. She helps find natural healing remedies and assists in channelling the energy of the moon in potions and crystals. You can call upon Haniel to add the company of wonderful friends to your life. She will help you answer your prayers and be receptive enough to receive those answers. She can add grace, harmony and beauty to our lives. She helps with feminine issues, such as menstrual cycles, PMS and the menopause.

Archangel Jeremiel

Jeremiel's name means 'mercy of God'. Calling upon Jeremiel can help when you are experiencing difficult times, and he will help you to see through situations. He helps you to forgive yourself and others. He helps us work with karma and releasing old patterns in life that are holding us back. He helps to put us back on the right path according to God's will, and to let go of regrets.

Archangel Metatron

The meaning of Metatron's name is not known. He is believed to be one of only two mortals who became angels (the other is Sandalphon). He is sometimes called the angel of presence. He is considered the youngest of the archangels because of his previous earthly existence (he lived his life as Enoch, who was a prophet and a scribe). He received the Sefer Raziel HaMalakh (the Book of Raziel the Angel). This book, which was given to Adam, Noah, Enoch, and finally Solomon, was said to have been created by Archangel Raziel. Jewish scholars called Metatron the 'angel of countenance'. This is because he witnesses the countenance of God and so extends God's word to humanity.

Enoch ascended as an angel to the highest level to live and work. He keeps records of everything on Earth and stores it in the Akashic records. Having once experienced an earthly life, he acts as an intermediary between Earth and Heaven and assists those who are in their earthly existence. He assists children, helping them to develop spiritual gifts, as well as helping those who have crossed over. He can also help newly developed people in deepening their spiritual gifts. When you call upon him he will help you in making bold choices and will give you motivation. Archangel

Metatron stands above the sacred circle.

Archangel Raguel

This angel's name means 'friend of God'. He assists with developing harmonious relationships. He oversees all the other archangels and angels and ensures that they are working harmoniously together. He is often referred to as the archangel of justice and fairness. He helps those who are doubted or trodden upon, to give them self-respect and empowerment. You can call upon him to resolve conflicts and to act as a mediator. Raguel is the angel who is credited with taking Enoch to heaven.

Archangel Raziel

This angel's name means 'secret of God'. This is because he is reputed to know the secrets of the universe. He created the Book of Raziel the Angel (see also Archangel Metatron). The origins of this book have been endlessly debated by scholars, but the book itself is difficult to understand and it is said that one must call upon Archangel Raziel in order to understand it.

This angel can assist in revealing to you secret esoteric knowledge. He can assist in the understanding of high-level knowledge, such as sacred geometry and quantum physics. He can help with your ability to access divine guidance. Calling upon him can help you deepen your spiritual practices and the understanding of them.

Archangel Sandalphon

This angel's name means 'brother' in Greek in reference to his 'twin' brother, Archangel Metatron, both of whom were originally mortal men. Sandalphon, in his earthly incarnation, was the prophet Elijah. Immortal assignments were given to both men for their earthly good work. Elijah was ascended to the heavenly realms in a fiery chariot led by two horses of fire, according to the Bible.

Sandalphon's main role is to take human prayers to God to be answered. He is said to extend from Earth to Heaven, as he is so tall. His messages may come to you as soft whispers or as music in your mind. He can be called upon to assist with music and creative endeavours. Archangel Sandalphon stands at the bottom of the sacred circle.

Other Beings of Light

Mary, Queen of Angels

Not much is known about Mary apart from what appears in the Gospels. In the Gospels, Mary lived in Nazareth along with her husband Joseph and son Jesus.

Mary was declared 'Queen of Angels' as she was the mother of Jesus. For early Christians and in the context of the Annunciation, this was how Mary gained the title. Mary had many interactions with angels in the Bible, most notably with Archangel Gabriel. Angels appear frequently as Mary's assistants, and early scholars such as Caesarius (c.1180–c.1240), suggested that her name could be called to overcome spiritual apparitions that were less than holy. If one encountered a fallen angel one could call her name to move it away (Keck, 1998).

There are many places where there have been visions of Mother Mary, such as Lourdes in France, Fátima in Portugal and Guadalupe in Mexico.

Babaji

Mahavatar Babaji appears in the book *Autobiography of a Yogi* by Paramhansa Yogananda. Babaji, according to the text, works closely with Jesus.

Lahiri Mahasaya was given the original Kriya Yoga by Babaji, and subsequently Yogananda spread the teachings to the Western world. Yogananda's book made Babaji known to the larger public, particularly in the Western world, for the first time.

Babaji is considered an immortal being who has appeared throughout the ages for the welfare and spiritual evolution of humanity (Siddhanath, 2012).

There are only certain details available of Babaji's life, as it is surrounded in mystery. It was at one time considered that the public at large were not ready to receive him. He has appeared to only a certain few devotees in physical form. Babaji works in total obscurity, and disciples are instructed to maintain a silence about him.

It is said that if you call his name three times he will be with you on the spiritual plane. He comes through as a warm, reassuring presence and encourages you to practise the asanas (poses) of hatha yoga. He works closely with Jesus.

According to Yogananda, Babaji resides in the Himalayas at no specific location. He has kept his physical form for possibly millennia.

In his book Yogananda states: 'The Mahavatar is in constant communion with Christ; together they send out vibrations of redemption, and they have planned the spiritual technique of salvation for this age. The work of these two fully illumined masters – one with the body and one without it – is to inspire the nations to forsake suicidal wars, race hatreds, religious sectarianism and the boomerang evils of materialism.' (Yogananda, 2015.)

'Truth, Simplicity and Love' —Haidakhan Babaji.

Quan Yin (Kuan Yin)

I have worked with Quan Yin extensively over the years. (There are variations on the spelling of her name. The spelling I use is the Chinese version.) There is a prayer to her included in the angelic prayers section. I often ask for her assistance in conjunction with the angels of the violet flame to transmute all negative energies. I also often use her when I am feeling nervous or anxious.

She comes in many different forms. She is traditionally the goddess of protection, mercy, and compassion with a deep unconditional love. She represents the feminine energy in Buddhism. She is sometimes depicted as holding a willow branch, a vase and occasionally a lotus flower. The willow branch is used to heal illnesses. The water contained in the vase is used to remove suffering, and represents purification.

Her energies sweep over you, giving a calming and reassuring presence, and she takes away any concerns or worries.

The Divine Circle

The angels of the divine circle can be used in protection, healing and conscious manifesting work. Request that the relevant angels attend the northern, southern, eastern and western quarters of the circle, with Sandalphon below and Metatron above. Ask the angels to return once the work is done and give thanks.

Working with the Archangels in Prayer and Healing

To enable a stronger connection with the major archangels their names can be intoned so that a greater connection with them is made. This can be true when intoning the names of the archangels with regard to the four directions or 'winds'.

This technique of intoning the names of the archangels for the four directions can be used to add a shield and light when conducting healing. Or it can be used when undertaking energetic work where the addition of the archangels will greatly enhance one's efforts, while adding protection and ensuring that the work is undertaken with the highest guidance possible. The directions for the archangels are taken from Christian Kabbalah, although some traditions place the angels at different directions.

The archangels of the four directions are as follows:

- East: Raphael
- West: Gabriel
- South: Michael
- North: Uriel.

There can also be the addition of Sandalphon below and Metatron above, making six angels in total. As with all work with the angelic realm, it can be a matter of individual choice. In the appendices there is an exercise in calling in the four winds (or four directions) that has been adapted from Gnostic healing practices.

In addition to this is a traditional bedtime prayer. This prayer describes the archangels of the four directions or winds. It asks for the protection and guidance during sleep. Part of the prayer is as follows:

To the right Michael and to my left Gabriel, in front of me Uriel and behind me Raphael, and above me the divine presence.

Chapter 4

The Angelic Hierarchy

In examining angels, and in identifying them in the Bible, it is practical to look at how the angels are organised. Biblical passages indicate that the angels are organised in terms of rank and glory. This idea of ranking angels may seem speculative, but it gives an idea of how angelic hierarchy is structured. It also helps us understand that there are angels that exist beyond those we already know about, such as guardian angels and archangels. The Bible indicates that the angelic beings had differing powers and authority and that the celestial beings were ranked accordingly. It indicates that some are closer to God, whereas others are closer to the human race and therefore more accessible, such as guardian angels and archangels.

The angelic hierarchy was passed down through the ages from Pseudo-Dionysius the Areopagite. For early thinkers the angelic hierarchy provided a way of explaining the hierarchical order of all creation.

According to Dionysius, the angels exist in three distinct hierarchies. Each hierarchy contains three separate orders (Keck, 1998).

The Angelic Hierarchy in Descending Order

First Hierarchy	Seraphim	(the names derive from their relationship to God)
	Cherubim	
	Thrones	
Second Hierarchy	Dominions	(the names all suggest a common administration or disposition for ordering the universe)
	Virtues	
	Powers	
Third Hierarchy	Principalities	(the names derive from the performance of their duties)
	Archangels	
	Angels	

The angels are grouped into the hierarchies or choirs, although there is much speculation about how these hierarchies were grouped. This hierarchy was put forward by Pseudo-Dionysius in his work *De Coelesti Hierarchia* (*On the Celestial Hierarchy*). Both Thomas Aquinas (in his work *Summa Theologica*) and Pseudo-Dionysius drew on passages from the New Testament in their attempts to reveal the angelic hierarchy.

The First Hierarchy

Seraphim

These are the highest order or choir of angels. They are mentioned in Isaiah 6:1–7 and Revelation 4–6. The word 'seraphim' comes from the Hebrew *saraph*, meaning 'to burn', or 'fiery flying serpent'. Seraphim are referred to as 'the burning ones' because they are ablaze for the love of God. They are described in Isaiah as having six pairs of wings: one pair for flying, one pair for covering their eyes (as even they cannot look at God) and one pair for covering their feet (believed to be a euphemism for their genitalia). They are described as having eyes all around, and are also described as hovering above the heavenly throne of God. Their duties are not clear, but they are constantly glorifying God. He can use these beings to purify and cleanse his servants.

Cherubim

Their name means 'fullness of knowledge'. They are considered guardians of God's glory and symbolise God's power and mobility. According to Ezekiel's vision, they have four faces: a man's face to the front, an eagle's face to the rear, an ox's face to the left and a lion's face to the right. He describes them as having four arms, each with a wing attached, with a pair of wings outstretched and the other pair covering the body. They are also defined as having feet and hands. Ezekiel also describes them as having wheels so that they could roll in any direction. Their image was incorporated into the design of the Ark of the Covenant. Both the cherubim and seraphim constantly glorify God and the cherubim sit at the side of God, according to the Bible. In Genesis 3:24 the cherubim are seen to guard the tree of life in the Garden of Eden.

Thrones or Ophanim

The word 'ophan' means 'wheel' in Hebrew. They are known as the chariots of God, and their role is to carry out God's justice in accordance with universal laws. Ezekiel described them as having their wheels covered in eyes. According to Catholic tradition the thrones are angels of humility, peace and submission. It is suggested that the lower choirs of angels need the thrones to access God.

The Second Hierarchy

Dominions

These are considered the angels of leadership in that they regulate the duties of the angels and make known the commands of God. They regulate the activities of the other angels except those in the first hierarchy. It is said that they are the angels that preside over nations. They are believed to look like beautiful humans with wings but are different from other angels in having an orb of light attached to their sceptres or to the pommel of their swords, which are symbols of their authority.

Virtues

Their primary duty is to oversee the heavenly bodies and ensure that the cosmos is in order. According to Catholic tradition they govern all nature, having control over the seasons, the stars, the moon and the sun. They provide courage, grace and valour, and are in charge of miracles.

Powers

The powers are said to work with the principalities. They are said to be warrior angels, defending the cosmos and humans against evil. The powers redress evil acts and protect human souls. They fight against evil spirits who attempt to wreak chaos through humans. They are the bearers of conscience and the keepers of history (the Akashic records). Their duty is to oversee the distribution of power among humankind.

The Third Hierarchy

Principalities

These angels work alongside the powers. They are the protectors of religion, and they provide strength in times of hardship. They are shown wearing a crown and bearing a sceptre. They oversee groups of people and large organisations of people, such as those in councils, hospitals, large companies and the like. They are said to inspire people in relation to (for example) art or science.

Archangels

Archangels are the angels that are most frequently referred to in the Bible. They have a unique role as God's messengers throughout history. Archangel Michael is considered to be the leader in this sphere of angels. Archangels are the chief angels, and as such look after the affairs of mankind. They are the holy messengers of God, carrying God's most important messages to humankind.

Angels

These are closest to human beings, and include guardian angels. They have the ability to access all other angelic realms. They deliver our prayers to God and respond with God's answers. They are concerned with all matters that affect people.

The idea of an angelic hierarchy has been passed down through the ages, from Pseudo-Dionysius the Areopagite onwards.

In trying to understand why we have hierarchies of angels it is good to understand where these ideas evolved from, rather than just presenting them and asking questions about where they come from and why.

Many of these ideas stem from medieval thinkers.

Hierarchies provided them with a way of explaining how all creation is structured.

In the scriptures there are references to a number of beings, such as seraphim, referred to by Isaiah. Cherubim appear in the Old Testament and in the writings of Saint Paul, who talks of principalities, powers, dominions and other beings. Angelic hierarchies were a way for the theologians of the time to understand these beings and to structure their realms in an ordered way. Luke 15:8–10 provided much scriptural basis for identifying the number nine as the number of angelic hierarchies (Keck, 1998).

The works of Pseudo-Dionysius appear to have been written around 500 AD. His angelic hierarchy became accepted in the Middle Ages and became part of the traditional Christian teachings at the time.

Chapter 5

Guardian Angels

Guardian angels rank the lowest of the nine orders of angels, according to traditional belief. Scholars and clerics asserted that humans have a guardian angel assigned to them at birth (some scholars suggest two). Winchester Cathedral contains a chapel that is dedicated to guardian angels. According to scripture, the names of guardian angels are incomprehensible to humans (Keck, 1998).

We all have a guardian angel. They are different from archangels as they are appointed to be with you throughout your life, possibly many lifetimes.

Guardian angels are there to support us on our spiritual journey through life and are responsible for taking our prayers up to God on our behalf. As with other spiritual beings of a similar nature, guardian angels cannot interfere with our free will choices. We must make a conscious effort to connect with our guardian angels and actively invite them into our lives. As with all angels they are neither male nor female, but you may wish to assign a gender to them. Angels are not gender-specific.

Your angel may come with a colour. Mine is pink.

Thomas Aquinas stated that a guardian angel was appointed to a person at birth and that until birth the mother's angel protected both mother and foetus (Keck, 1998).

After reading Matthew 18:10, Acts 12:15 and Tobit 3:25, the clerics contended that a person would have an angel watch each individual soul as ordained by God. Saint Bonaventure argued that having a guardian angel did not affect free will but that they assisted in spiritual effort. Both Thomas Aquinas and Saint Bonaventure agreed that a person cannot lose their guardian angel (ibid.).

As previously stated, it was believed that the names of guardian angels are not intelligible and are difficult for humans to understand. In fact when I once had a reading with a medium my guardian angel appeared to the medium, but she could not understand the name given. I have struggled to get the name of my guardian angel but have an agreed version of it. Your guardian angel may give you a simple name to call them by. Your guardian angel will never leave you and will constantly be by your side.

When connecting with your guardian angel, ask them for a sign. This could be a physical sign of their presence, such as the gentle pulling of an ear or blowing, or you could ask them to give you a symbol each day.

When I first started working with the angels I asked

to be given a symbol to work with. Sure enough, I would wake up with a symbol each morning that I would record in my journal. I then researched the symbol or meditated on it.

When you connect with your guardian angel they may 'speak' to you in a different way from how a spirit guide might. They may communicate in a rather old-fashioned way or impress imagery into your subconscious to convey their message. You may have an impression put into your mind, such as a sense of urgency to complete a specific task. Trust your guidance. Your guardian angel may, as mine does often, guide you to books, courses or even crystals.

If you have difficulty with another person you can connect your guardian angel with their guardian angel to try to resolve the issue. I have done this myself with amazing results. In the section in this book about Padre Pio you will see that he regularly sent his guardian angel out to undertake healing work and often requested that people sent their guardian angels to him for the same. In this way he could perform the healings without having to receive too many visitors or having to leave the monastery where he resided.

You too can use your guardian angel to resolve issues as they arrive. On many occasions when there have been problems or possible conflict at work I have asked my guardian angel to soothe the issue or to guide my speech or actions so that I can solve the problem to the best of my ability. This is especially useful when situations are particularly stressful and there could be the possibility of a flare-up.

As angels resonate on a different, higher vibration, it is good to raise your vibrational energy to elevate it towards that of the angelic realms in order to get the best angelic communication. Traditionally this would have been done by the use of prayer. By sitting in meditation and consciously raising your vibration upwards you will enhance your connection to your guardian angel. (We will look more at raising vibrational energy in a later chapter.)

Angelic communication gets easier the more you practise it. Your guardian angel may indicate their presence by a feeling of warmth, a gentle push or pressure (perhaps on the back), a gentle blow, a feeling of cobwebs on your face or a gentle tugging of your ears. Any of these sensations may be indicative of angelic communication. You can agree with your guardian angel that when they are around they communicate their presence with a specific feeling or sensation.

Your angel may leave clues that they are around – for example, white feathers. Whenever I see a white feather I know that angels are around. The first time I visited Mother Shipton's Cave in Knaresborough, North Yorkshire, England there were feathers scattered over the path to her cave. I had never seen so many feathers on a path before. I knew that my guardian angels were with me that day, guiding me. (Mother Shipton was a famous prophetess and healer who lived in the north of England in the fifteenth century.)

Your guardian angel may visit you at night while you

are sleeping. I've woken many times in the night with a sense of an angelic presence in my room. It is always a comforting sensation and never scary. An angelic presence will always feel loving and supportive and will never cause fear. On one occasion I sensed two beings of light come through my bedroom window and float into my bedroom in the middle of the night. The spheres of light lit up my room. It was an experience I will never forget.

Sometimes my guardian angel will be close by and I will sense a buzzing sensation in my ear. If I need to I will ask my guardian angel to come closer into my aura or to give me a clear sign of what my angel is trying to convey to me.

When my guardian angel is close by I will feel a gentle pressure on the top of my shoulder blades and into the back of my head. I am feeling this sensation now as I write this passage, so I know that my guardian angel is guiding me as I write. You may experience similar sensations when you connect with your angels.

Connecting with Your Guardian Angel through Automatic Writing

There is more on automatic writing in a further chapter, but here is a nice exercise to use. This following exercise can also work well if you wish to commune with your spirit guide or any other high-dimensional beings. Ask that any beings you connect with are of 100 per cent light and of peace. I have had a lot of success with this, and some of the communication I have received has gone into my writing.

Sit upright in a comfortable chair where you will not be disturbed. Ensure your feet are flat on the floor and your limbs are not crossed. You may wish to put on some background music (that has no words) and perhaps burn some incense.

Close your eyes and take a few long, deep breaths and feel your feet connect to the floor. Visualise roots like the roots of a tree emerging from the soles of your feet, grounding you. Let go of any thoughts as you quieten your mind.

See your aura expand outwards and upwards as you consciously raise your vibration to connect with your guardian angel. You may wish to ask for a sign to confirm that your guardian angel is with you. Take a few moments to connect.

When you are ready, pick up your pen and paper. Begin to write. You might start this process by writing a greeting to your angel or writing down a question. Ask for a divinely guided message. Start writing what comes to you. It doesn't matter if at first it doesn't make sense. Eventually it will. Write for as long as you feel inspired to do so.

When you have finished give thanks for your communication. Know that each time you do this exercise it will become easier for the words to flow. Put the pen and paper down. Consciously disconnect, seal and protect your energy field in a bubble of light.

When you have finished look over what you have written. You may be surprised at the insights you have been given.

The more you do this exercise the easier it gets.

Angel Signs

Guardian angels are powerful beings of light and are constantly in our presence, whether we are aware of it or not. There are various ways in which our angels can communicate with us, and these are ways we might not necessarily be aware of. Sometimes their communication can be by using subtle signs to show that they are nearby. These signs can come from all angels, whether they are guardian angels or archangels.

Angels communicate in many ways. Sometimes this is directly, and sometimes it is with physical signs. As I have already mentioned, when I first visited Mother Shipton's Cave my path to the cave was strewn with feathers. I had never seen so many feathers. At first I thought that maybe a bird had been caught by a predator, as there were so many of them. Then, as I walked further through the park woodland towards the cave, I saw more and more feathers. I tried to rationalise why there would be so many feathers but I just couldn't. I knew that my angels were near, giving me signs of their presence. Maybe it was even Mother Shipton herself.

Angels will give many signs to show that they are present. These signs and indicators give reassurance that their angelic presence is nearby. One of these signs is seeing feathers. Yes, perhaps a bird has been flying nearby and dropped a feather, but if your awareness is drawn to feathers on your path they can be interpreted as a sign from your angels. Next time you are walking, ask for a sign from the angels and you may see a feather on your path (or many, as I did).

Seeing flashes of light nearby are also signs that angels are near. I often see flashes of light just in the corner of my eye. Just recently, when writing a chapter for this book, I saw a very distinct bright flash of light just to the right side of my peripheral vision, almost like a spark from striking a flint or a lit sparkler. It was so bright that I couldn't dismiss it as my imagination and automatically knew that it was a sign from my angels.

I also regularly see coloured orbs. Again, they are so obvious that I could not mistake them for anything except the presence of angels nearby. When my mother-in-law was very ill and close to dying I regularly saw deep purple orbs appearing in front of me, about six feet away. I knew that they were a sign from a spirit, but at that time I didn't make the connection to the angels. Soon after this she died and I didn't start to see orbs again until months later, when I began to invite angels into my life. Now I regularly see orbs of various colours and I know that each colour represents an angel. They are there to give reassurance that an angel is nearby.

Another way in which angels may communicate with you is through dreams. One night when I was asleep, in the early hours of the morning, I was awoken to the sound of a voice repeating a particular phrase. I knew that it was important so I got up and grabbed my pen and journal, which I always have at the side of my bed in a drawer. I wrote down the phrase. It was subsequently used in my first book and was used at the back for my book blurb. It is always good to have a journal by your bedside, together with a pen, so that when the angels do come to you with words, phrases or visions you can write them down as I did. This is something that I continue to do.

Finding Your Life's Purpose

Once you connect fully with your guardian angel they will help guide you to your life's purpose if you allow them to do so. When you align to your life's purpose your life will become more harmonious. Synchronicities will begin to appear. Opportunities, people and events will begin to materialise that will help put you on to the path of self-realisation (the fulfilment of your own potential).

These changes might not be sudden. They may be subtle changes, easing you along your life's journey. You may be compelled to make life changes: give up addictive substances, become vegetarian, practise yoga, start to make healthier life choices. You might seek out like-minded people, learn new skills, become a healer, teach others. You may desire to give angel readings, work with crystals or essential oils, meditate more. You may sense things that once gave you pleasure, such as whiling away your hours in the pub or watching endless hours of television, seem empty and fall away. You may find yourself wanting to live your life in a more constructive and meaningful way.

Your guardian angel's divine mission is to guide you to your life purpose, the reason why you were set on this earth. Angels can set you on a course to self-realisation, to a greater connection to the source, to the universal consciousness you call God. You might notice these synchronicities and notice events unfolding as they serve some divine plan.

When you know that you are here ready for a purpose, you should align your thoughts and ideas so that they are in balance with what you wish to set out to do. Allow the universal law of attraction to align with your being and know that the universe is co-creating to allow people and opportunities that will assist you in manifesting your divine purpose in life. See this divine plan unfold and allow it to do so. Be in a state of allowing. Do not force it, but at the same time be sure to take action steps towards your goal. Don't force things if resistance or obstacles occur. Those obstacles might be there for a reason. Take time to check in with your own intuition. Ask the angels and the divine beings and go with what feels right.

Know and feel the universe coming together, aligning with your soul's purpose – the reason why you are here on this earth – and allow the divine plan put before you to unfold. When you are aligned with your life's purpose you will feel joy and enthusiasm in following your path. Actively feel the universe conspiring to offer you the wondrous opportunities needed so that you can fulfil your mission in life.

Finding my life's purpose was something that evaded me for years. I had a rough idea of what my life's purpose was, but it was something that just didn't seem to manifest for me. When I listened to spiritual call-in shows online, or read spiritual books, the most frequently asked question seemed to be, 'How do I find my life's purpose?'

It came to a point when I realised that I had to stop searching for the answers and asking the same old questions, like, 'Should I do this? Should I do that?' Instead I had to take a step back and somehow put myself into a place of faith and trust in the universe, with the knowledge that I was exactly where I was meant to be, doing exactly what I was meant to do. I felt that life would unfold exactly as it should, while simultaneously I knew that I needed to consciously align myself to my life's purpose and that it would reveal itself in due course.

Prior to this I had spent many years chasing what I thought I should be doing, and it always ended in disaster. Things began to take shape when I took a step back and allowed the universe to work its power, and I asked the angels for guidance and assistance and to direct me to my life's purpose. Things began to manifest with more ease once I aligned myself into a state of allowing. This did not mean that I was lazy and didn't look for opportunities coming my way. Rather, I began to allow events to reveal themselves instead of trying to force things. If something wasn't meant to be or circumstances were stacking up against me I would take a step back and let things unfold in time. I also had to learn patience.

My life changed dramatically when I allowed the angels into my life. I realised that I needed to allow events to unfold rather than constantly chase them. I needed to step back from my ego self and allow the universe and the divine source to work their magic, and I enlisted the help of angelic guidance.

You have a unique purpose in life, and this is why you have been set upon this earth. You perhaps will never be a millionaire or invent a life-changing gadget, but you are here to fulfil a divine purpose. That's what we are all here for. Align your being with the divine source, enlist the help of the angels and allow events to unfold as if guided by a divine hand. Your purpose may be to help others, to teach, to heal or to inspire.

I'm a massive fan of the late Dr Wayne Dyer. In his book *The Power of Intention* (2010) he has ten steps for living your life so that you align to your soul's purpose. I have summarised them as follows:

1. No one shows up by accident, not even you. There is meaning to your existence. Know that you are here on purpose.
2. Live your life in service to others. Let go of the ego and help others along the way. If it is your purpose to be a mother, put all your energy into your children. If it's fixing teeth, put all your energy into making people look the best they can. Make a difference to others and let the universe take care of the details. Live in joy and gratitude.

74

3. Align yourself to your purpose. Have faith that the universe knows your purpose even if you don't. Know that your purpose will be revealed and have faith.

4. Ignore what others may say that your life purpose should be. This is your life, not theirs. Listen to your own heart.

5. Remember that the field of intention will work on your behalf. The universe supports life. See it as friendly, not hostile. See it working for you, not against you.

6. Act as if you were living the life you were intended to live. Act as though you are living a purposeful life (this doesn't mean spending above your means). Treat obstacles as opportunities to test your resolve and to find your life's purpose.

7. Study the lives of people who know their life's purpose and replicate that. Read about inspirational people you admire and how they were motivated to stay on purpose. There are many motivational speakers with videos and books about this.

8. Meditate to stay on purpose. Dyer recommended Japa meditation (meditating on the word of God or 'Ahh'). Meditation, even for just a few moments a day, will set your intention. I meditate each morning to set my intentions for the day ahead and I also take time to connect with divine guidance.

9. Keep feelings and thoughts in line with actions.

Check your thoughts. If you are in disharmony it will take you away from your purpose. Keep thoughts positive and harmonious.

10. Keep a state of gratitude. Be thankful for opportunities and obstacles. See everything from a perspective of gratitude: jobs, successes, people, failures. Everything puts you on the path of your life's purpose. You're here for a reason and that is to be purposeful. Be thankful. There is much to be grateful for.

Taken from *The Power of Intention* (2010) by Dr Wayne Dyer.

These points summarise for me what needs to be done to align to your life's purpose and for it to manifest. It's not an easy task, but these little pointers help me stay on track and remind me what I should be doing. I hope they do the same for you.

Chapter 6

Raising Your Spiritual Vibration

The Path of Least Resistance

This term comes from the late Wayne Dyer and is referred to in one of my favourite books of his, *The Power of Intention* (2010).

This term specifically refers to living in the now. The shape and quality of your thoughts, Dyer explains, can put up resistant thoughts. Aligning your thoughts to what is creative, positive, tranquil and peaceful, while also letting go of stress, helps raise your vibrational energy. Once the vibrations are lifted this then allows your creative processes to formulate themselves. In making positive lifestyle choices to raise our vibrational energies we can ultimately develop a better connection with the angels and receive higher guidance from them.

We live in an abundant universe, and at a time when we can create whatever we choose. We have the world at our fingertips and knowledge that can be accessed in an instant, yet many of us reside in despair, experience negative thought processes, and put up resistance to allow all that is good into our lives.

Writing and using positive affirmations can help raise our vibrations. This will allow creative energy to develop while aligning those creative processes to the universe. The use of positive affirmations can help change thought patterns.

An affirmation is a verbal description of the desired condition that you wish to achieve and can be used to create the reality that we require. Affirmations should be positive and in the present tense and preferably short, so that they can be remembered. Raising your vibrations through positive intention and letting go of all the things that no longer work for you will give you an inner peace.

Living aligned to the moment, to the now, is imperative in being able to develop this process of acquiring peace. All that exists is this moment, the now. The future has not yet arrived, and may arrive in ways that you could never have expected. Yes, you are a product of all those past experiences that you have had, but they are just that: past experiences. You cannot change them. Accept that the events that have happened in your life have brought you to the point where you are today. The past cannot be any different from what it was. There are lessons that you can take from it, but there is little point in believing that things could be any different from what they were. What has happened is just that: experiences and events that have happened in the past. The past should not be allowed to hold on to you as a prisoner of your own thoughts. Sometimes the storms in life come not to disrupt your life but to clear the path for new and better experiences.

Forgiveness has a role in this concept. It is about accepting that what has happened and how you can move on from those experiences. It's about how can you make your life better despite those experiences.

When I reflect on certain events that have happened in my life I look back at them and give thanks. I give thanks to those events and experiences, as they made me into the person that I am today. However, those events don't define me as a person. They don't wholly dictate my life, and I don't dwell on them. I take the lessons that I have learnt from them and move forward.

The now is all there ultimately is. There will be a future, but it is not here yet. But what you do in this moment, how you live your life, can influence the paths you take in the future. So make it good, and by being good you can make yourself an instrument of peace. By being peaceful you can align yourself to your divine purpose, the reason why you are here.

By feeling bad you can create an anxious state, resistant to allowing positive changes. By aligning to positive thoughts and feelings you can align to the divine creative state, the state of allowing and being. By allowing yourself to realise your full potential as a human being you can become a beacon of hope for others, a shining light and an inspiration. Live fully in the moment to all you have now. Make the choice to feel good about yourself and others and the world around you.

Low energy thoughts weaken our positive intentions and restrict us from attracting what we desire. We are what we think about. If we dwell on past issues and mistakes, on events in our lives and on thoughts of fear and shame, this will manifest itself in lowering our spiritual energies. Those lower vibrational energies may then in turn be acted out by acts of being unkind and uncaring and by taking out our resentments on others around us, including those who we love. When you are kind to others you receive kindness back. When you treat others with anger and hurt you receive those energies back too.

The more you align yourself with positive intent the more the universe will provide you with the opportunities that align to your soul's purpose. To stay in harmony with the energetic influences that surround you, align your thoughts in conjunction with your divine nature. When you do this the more positively, the better the universe will respond.

Your divine nature is to be at peace, to live in a positive manner, to live in harmony with nature, to be in balance, and not to react to stress in a negative way.

When you align yourself to your true nature – your divine purpose – you will manifest great things. It is essential not to enter into conflict with this true essence of your being. Don't work against it. Non-harmonious energy comes from non-harmonious

80

thoughts and feelings. When we are harmonious our energy level will naturally be elevated and our spiritual vibrations will be lifted.

When we naturally elevate our thoughts and feelings we can commune more easily with higher vibrational beings, such as angels. Without inner harmony and peace it makes it difficult to hear our inner voice, the voice of our soul. If we can't connect with our inner voice we can't hear the voices of elevated spiritual beings or of God.

As Wayne Dyer says in his book: As you practise being in a state of allowing and living a life of least resistance, success is what you become, not what you choose. It becomes what you are, your natural state of being. Abundance will no longer evade you, it will flow to you unimpeded (Dyer, 2010).

Know and feel abundance as part of your natural state of being.

Gratitude

Cultivating gratitude is an acquired skill. In a recent study it was found that adults who participated in a gratitude letter-writing exercise experienced significant improvements in their mental health. Many studies have found that people who make a conscious effort to count their blessings tend overall to be less depressed, and happier.

Think of someone you know who complains all the time. How do they make you feel?

Gratitude for what we have is something that tends

to be overlooked. We can find ourselves focusing on the negatives rather than focusing on the positives. Instead, focusing on and expressing gratitude for what we do have – rather than on what we don't have – can bring about a more peaceful state. By expressing gratitude, we take away the focus from what we don't have and the stress and frustration that that brings. Expressing gratitude brings us into alignment with our authentic selves.

Once gratefulness begins to be embedded as part of daily practice and gratitude is given for what we have in life, the law of attraction takes effect.

What we give out, we receive. Positive thoughts attract positive energies into our everyday existence. Gratitude is a vital element of success. Being grateful can eliminate some of the negative thoughts that can permeate daily life. Gratitude also brings more meaning to life. When you live in a state of gratitude the positive attitude it brings permeates through your life, and in turn attracts positive people and experiences.

Be grateful for everything in your life: your shower in the morning, the daily sunrise, the journey to work, your job, the food on the table, the weather, whatever money you have in your pocket, your family and your kids. The list is endless. It allows you to be in a state of mindfulness, to be aware of the possibilities, and it takes away some of the burdens of life.

At times, while on the way to work and wishing that I could be at home doing different things, I used to think to myself, 'I hate my job.' Most of us have been there. I changed that statement to, 'I am grateful for my job and the money it pays so that I can enjoy the nicer things in life.' My attitude to work changed, and I was happier and more successful at my work as a result. Instead of putting up a resistance to my work in actively hating it, by changing my thought processes I worked with it rather than against it. As Dyer constantly said, 'Change the way you look at things, and the things you look at change'.

Making a conscious effort to express gratitude can pay dividends. Gratitude can make us happier, can improve health and relationships. Gratitude also reduces materialism and the need to hang on to stuff, and can help make us less self-centred and selfish.

Write down what you are grateful for in a journal. Cultivating gratitude as a daily practice will bring you peace of mind and contentment, and will help elevate your vibrational energies.

Connecting with the Divine Essence that is Love

Love brings us back to the source of all that is and all that can ever be. The greatest essence there is on this earth is love: the love of your partner, your family, your companions and your pets.

When you see people and step in, judging the way they are or the way they look, take time to reflect that they are part of the divine source – the same as you. Remember that no one is imperfect. Look to replace those thoughts, and bring them back into alignment with the divine. Replace those thoughts with those of love.

Ask the angels to assist and to help you connect with the divine source that is God, and surround your being with love and divine harmony.

When you judge others, perhaps you are also judging yourself or are reflecting other people's previous judgements of you. Take time to check in with those thoughts and turn them to love. Ask the angels to assist in surrounding you with love and loving thoughts.

When you judge someone to be fat, dirty or unkempt, or look down on them because they are not the same as you, take time to reflect that those people have had experiences in their lives that have brought them to the point where they are today. Seek to find opportunities to replace judgemental and limiting thoughts with love and compassion. Seek to see inspiration and love in all manner of things. Extend that love outwards, and love will be reciprocated to you.

There are no greater words than 'I love you'.

Replace contemptuous thoughts with those of love and compassion through connecting with the heart centre. If you struggle, ask the angels to assist in turning your thoughts and deeds to those of love and compassion.

Love is all around us. We just need to see it, tap into it. Love is a magnificent force that can change people's lives beyond what they ever perceived possible. Love is the glue that connects us, holds us together.

Love also begins with the self. Your physical body is a part of the divine source. It is beautiful and perfect, so treat it as sacred. Tend to it with care. Make improvements by nourishing it with healthy, wholesome food. Purge it of toxins and give it some love. Express the radiance of abundant love through every pore of your being, from inside out. We are all perfect in our own imperfections. Express your being through the act of love.

Surround yourself with angelic love. Feel it radiate outward, and sense it coming back to you in droves.

Your soul is your garden. Tend to it daily and feed it with love.

Crystals

When I was a small child I loved to pick up smooth and unusual stones wherever I went. I would collect them on my walks in nature and pop them in various places in my bedroom. I had a natural tendency to collect stones because I knew that they were gifts from nature and that somehow they gave off a certain energy, but I did not understand how or why. When I look at many of these stones that I collected, most of them now placed in my garden, I can see that they have natural quartz inclusions in them.

I spent hours when I was very young with my friend and her mother on the nearby disused railway near my home, scouring through the pebbles on the track for unusual stones and ones that contained fossils. My fascination carried on as I got older and my knowledge expanded, and I have collected various types of crystals over the years. I love to use them to lift energies in the home, to elevate my own emotions, for self-healing and to enhance my meditations.

Crystals resonate at a particular frequency and contain piezoelectric properties. When compressed they can produce electricity and sometimes light.

Crystals are wonderful at lifting energies – not just your own energies, but also in the home. Where there is any stagnant energy in the house, or a spot that needs uplifting, place a crystal there.

Clear quartz is one of the most common and most versatile crystals to use. Rose quartz is a pink quartz that gives off a subtle energy, and is known as a stone of love. I have a bed of amethyst, which is a lovely powerful and protective stone, on my sideboard. I also have a bed of citrine, which is a self-cleansing stone, and I have a large chunk of citrine placed in the left-hand corner of my home for money luck. I also have a small piece in my purse for the same reason, as citrine is a stone of prosperity. These are just some examples of the stones and crystals that I have dotted about my home. Plus I have various items of crystal jewellery that I wear. My most special piece is a moldavite pendant set in silver. Moldavite is a very powerful and spiritual stone that is said to have extraterrestrial origins. It was formed when a meteorite struck the earth.

Crystals are wonderful at lifting energies and consciousness, and are especially useful when working with the angelic realm. They are wonderful to hold while meditating. Alternatively you can carry them in your pocket to uplift you during the day, or you can use crystals for healing purposes.

Choosing Crystals

There is a saying that you do not choose crystals. They choose you. If you go into a crystal shop and are constantly drawn to a particular crystal, then that is the one for you. It is best to pick whichever crystal you are drawn to, rather than have a specific crystal in mind.

Use your intuition and inner guidance when choosing crystals. If you are struggling to decide what crystal to choose, ask the angels to give you guidance. You will also find, as I have, that crystals will be gifted to you by friends and family. I once bought a skull-shaped crystal from someone who insisted that one day when she was meditating with it that the crystal had indicated that it needed a new owner, and subsequently that was me.

If you do wish to buy a crystal for a specific purpose, use a crystal directory or use an online resource. The crystal that speaks to you is the right one. If you are purchasing from an online store do check out their returns policy, so that if isn't suitable you can return it.

When purchasing from a shop, handle several crystals and pick the one(s) that make you tingle or you feel you have a strong connection with. Use angelic guidance. Don't shy away from rough crystals (ones that are not polished). They still have very effective energies.

Cleansing Crystals

When you have chosen your crystal it will need cleansing. However, some crystals, such as selenite, are porous and are not suitable to cleanse in water, so check. I once ruined a beautiful hand-made turquoise ring by keeping it on when washing the dishes, so it's important to ensure that your crystals won't be damaged by water.

Crystals need cleansing if they have been given to you and also when they are newly purchased. If they have been used for healing work they also need to be cleansed before using again. Crystals absorb negative energies and so need regular cleansing. There are some, though, that are self-cleansing, such as citrine, azeztulite and kyanite. A bed of citrine can be used to lay small crystals on top to cleanse them.

Crystals can be kept in pouches of velvet or silk when not in use, to keep them protected. Velvet pouches can easily be purchased very cheaply from New Age shops or online.

Crystals can be cleansed under running water (a stream or a tap) or put into a bowl of water containing salt overnight. Ensure that the crystals are rinsed of any salt. And, again, check that the crystal is not porous and can't be damaged by being left in water. On the other hand, crystals can be left out under a full moon. Alternatively, they can be smudged by being passed over smoke from a smouldering sage stick or from some incense. As you pass the crystal through the smoke hold the intention that the smoke is cleansing the crystal of all negative energies.

Some Useful Crystals

There is a huge wealth of crystals on the market, and there are far too many to list in this chapter. However, these are some of my favourite crystals. If you wish to learn about crystals in more depth I recommend any book by crystal expert Judy Hall.

Agate	A grounding and balancing stone. Soothing and calming. Heals inner anger. Good for emotional trauma. Raises consciousness and encourages assimilation of life experiences.
Amethyst	A powerful and protective stone. Transmutes negative energies. A spiritual stone. Enhances spiritual awareness and aids meditation. Good for overcoming addictions. Helpful for insomnia, memory and motivation.
Angelite	A stone of awareness. Facilitates contact with the angelic realms. Aids telepathy and out-of-body journeying. Assists with attaining peace and tranquillity.
Aventurine	Good for geopathic stress and for prosperity. Calms negative situations. Relieves stammers, anxiety and fears. Promotes feelings of well-being.

Bloodstone	Cleanses the blood. Believed to possess magical and mystical properties. Gets rid of negativity. Helps with mental processes.
Carnelian	A stabilising stone that is good for motivation and creativity. Gives courage, protection and good concentration.
Citrine	An energising stone and a good cleanser. Transmutes negative energies and attracts abundance, success and prosperity. A joyful stone, and good for overcoming fears and phobias.
Clear Quartz.	Powerful healing stone. Works on all levels. Dispels negativity. A good all-round stone. Amplifies energy, enhances psychic attributes, and aids concentration and memory.
Fluorite	Good for psychic protection. Dispels negative energies and overcomes disorganisation. Can help with spiritual awakening. Promotes structure, gets rid of chaos, and is stabilising.
Hematite	A grounding and protective stone. Gets rid of negativity. Balancing. Good for addictions, for getting rid of limitations. Good for the blood.
Jasper	Good for stress and protection, and assists with balancing emotions and grounding. A good stone for healing. Helps with courage and shamanic journeying.

Labradorite	A mystical stone. Raises consciousness and gets rid of negative energies. Enhances psychic abilities and aids intuition. Gets rid of insecurities and fear.
Lapis Lazuli	Stimulates psychic abilities. Gets rid of stress and gives peace. A protective stone, and gives harmony. Good for communication.
Moldavite	A rare stone that enhances communication with the higher self and with spiritual dimensions. Good for meditation and for balancing the mind and body.
Moonstone	A stone of intuition. Calms the emotions, and can help with clairvoyance. Helps balance emotions, and is nurturing and calming.
Rose Quartz	A stone of unconditional love and peace. Opens the heart to love, forgiveness and compassion. Helps with positive affirmations. A good stone for midlife crises.
Selenite	A stone for angelic communication. Excellent for meditation and spiritual work. Good for relieving stress, and assists in gaining good judgement and insight. Dissolves in water.
Smoky Quartz	A grounding and protective stone. Relieves stress. Brings calmness. Promotes concentration and neutralises fearful thoughts. Excellent for meditation and communication.

Sodalite	Good for meditating. Calms and clears the mind. Helps get rid of old mental conditioning and can help alleviate phobias, fears and guilt.
Tiger's Eye	A protective stone, traditionally used to ward off evil wishes and curses. Gives clearer perception and insight. Good for resolving inner conflicts. Enhances psychic abilities.
Tourmaline	Transmutes dense energies. A shamanic stone. Good for protection. A powerful healing stone. Enhances inspiration, tolerance and compassion, and attracts prosperity.
Turquoise	A powerful protection and healing stone. Aids in communication in the spiritual and physical worlds. Dispels negative energy. Calms the nerves when public speaking. Brings inner calm.

Chapter 7

The Aura – A Life Force Energy Field

As we develop spiritually we need to be aware of how the energy field that surrounds our body is affected by the substances we eat and drink. This vibrational energy field is more commonly known as the aura. Everything that we eat and drink contains a life force energy and can affect our vibrational energy or aura. When we are on the spiritual path we should want our vibrational energy to be at its peak. We all have weaknesses. For some it is chocolate, for others alcohol or caffeine. We need to be aware, however, that substances such as these can affect our life force energy.

When you are following the spiritual path you may find that your need for such substances falls away naturally, and you will seek out more high vibrational foods and substances. Indeed, changing your diet and the way you live will not only have a positive effect on your health but it will also lift your emotions, help you deal with challenges that occur in a more constructive way and reduce the impact of negative emotions, such as anger. You may also find that as you develop spiritually you may become more sensitive to substances that are bad for you.

Things to avoid are caffeine, alcohol, cigarettes, chocolate, red meat, drugs, heavily processed foods and foods that have been genetically modified. Foods to consume more of are fruit and vegetables (preferably organic), whole grains, alternative sources of meat and dairy products such as soy and tofu, and a generally more plant-based diet. You can ask the angels to help guide you to the foods that will have a more positive effect.

Using Visualisation to Strengthen and Protect the Auric Field

When we begin to open up spiritually we can become more sensitive to the energies, both negative and positive, around us. We encounter many energy fields during the day, including electrical fields that surround items such as computers and mobile phones, and these can affect and interact with our own energy field. We may come across people who are emotionally demanding or draining, people who are generally negative or angry, or we may work in stressful environments that are harmful to our emotional and physical well-being. Unfortunately many of these things can't be avoided. Even our own thought patterns or behaviour can be negative. Protecting and strengthening our auric field becomes essential as we encounter these various energies during our day.

The section about white light meditation in Appendix 2 is an excellent visualisation to use in strengthening and protecting your auric field. Just like your physical body, your aura (the energy field that surrounds your body) needs to be cleansed from time to time. The exercise can be completed in the morning to set you up for the day ahead or may be used at the end of the day to get rid any negative energies you have encountered. You may also find that it assists in getting a better night's sleep.

Another good way is to have a ritual bath. Adding a handful of Epsom salts (magnesium sulphate crystals) to your bathwater is a good way to cleanse the auric field, or you can sprinkle a handful of unrefined natural sea or rock salt into your bath. Epsom salts are cheap to buy. When put in a bath they help in the removal of toxins and can help to relax the body and mind.

Make it a spiritual experience. Invite your angels to help you let go of anything not of peace. You may wish to light candles or use pure essential oils to add aromas. A few drops of essential oil added to your bathwater can also have healing and relaxation qualities. Soak for around twenty minutes, or longer if you wish. Visualise the water cleansing your aura and taking away all that negative spiritual debris you have picked up during the day, in addition to cleansing you physically. Make sure that you rest fully after your bath, and drink plenty of water. If you don't have a bath visualise the water from a shower cleansing away all the negativity. In addition, if you are a reiki practitioner you can use your symbols as well.

Using these techniques can help keep the negative debris we encounter daily under control. The more positive we feel about ourselves the more positive experiences we can attract in our daily life.

Smudging

Using bundles of sage to spiritually cleanse spaces, particularly in the home, is a great way to lift vibrational energies and clear away any stuck or dense energies. If you play violent video games, watch violent things on television or have arguments in the home, they can all leave a negative spiritual residue. Although these energies don't stop the angels coming into your life, regular spiritual cleansing can help raise your vibrational energy. You know yourself if you enter a room after there has been an argument in it you can probably feel the dense energy there, and it may make you feel uncomfortable.

Begin by setting the intention to cleanse the home of negative energy by the act of smudging. Objects such as crystals can also be cleansed this way by passing the item through the smoke and visualising the negative energy being removed. You can also cleanse people by passing the smoke around the auric field.

To do this, light the end of the smudge stick and blow out the flame. Put the smudge stick on a plate to catch any burning embers or on an abalone shell. Waft the smoke using either your hand or a feather fan. You may have to blow on the smudge stick regularly to produce more smoke. As you go around the home visualise the smoke from the smudge stick removing all negative vibrations and stuck energy, leaving only positive energies.

The Aura and the Environment

Everything in the universe is made up of energy, and you vibrate at a certain frequency (as does everything around you). This energy is constantly flowing and moving. As we go about our daily lives we interact with different energy fields, different moods and emotions, different environments. The energy in an office is very different from the energy out in nature, for example. Everything vibrates at a specific frequency (as do tables, chairs and doors (and everything else), even though they are solid).

We interact with various energetic fields, which emanate from items such as mobile phones, computers, mechanical equipment and lighting. As we go about our day we encounter many things that drain our energy, including electrical fields that may be invisible, such as those from computers and mobile phones. In fact any appliance that is connected to a mains electricity supply will give off electrical and magnetic fields while it is working. If we are mindful of this we will notice the effects that working near or passing through these electrical fields will have, and how they can affect our vibrational field.

We interact with many different people with different moods, emotions and personalities during our day. Some we encounter we may even unwittingly enter into conflict with, or we may come across people who are anxious or stressed. The day may have started out perfectly but after the commute to work, a stressful day at the office and the journey back home to family life, our resolve may feel weakened. The stress and negativity encountered through the day can inadvertently have an effect on our own energetic levels and bring them down during the course of the day.

Your vibrational frequency emanates from your thoughts, emotions and actions. Our alignment to the universe and our vibrational frequencies dictate what we attract. A higher vibrational state that is more positive in nature will attract more uplifting experiences and people.

Food and Drink

The role of diet is very important in keeping our energies high, and it is good to be mindful of the foods and substances we take into our bodies.

Many of us are guilty of eating junk food: crisps, chips or fries, sodas, alcohol… The list goes on. Eating more of high vibrational foods can elevate our mood and make us feel better.

Everything that we eat or drink contains a life force energy. Certain foods, such as junk food, have a lower life force energy, whereas other foods, such as fresh vegetables, wholefoods and organic produce, have a higher life force energy. Eating more of the higher life force energy foods can help with raising your own vibrational energies and improve your health.

Cutting back on foods and substances that are bad, such as alcohol, caffeine, tobacco, red meat and drugs, can all assist in improving your overall health and raising your vibrational levels. Other foods that can be eaten more moderately which affect your vibrational fields are processed foods, products made with white flour, foods with a high sugar content, sodas and dairy products. A plant-based diet with organically grown produce (where possible) and drinking more water will assist in improving your health and well-being. Even the smallest of changes can be beneficial to raising your vibrational energies.

Exercise

Exercise is not only beneficial to your health and well-being but it can also elevate your energies and your mood. Any type of aerobic exercise that has you breathing more rapidly will increase your energy flow. Yoga is also good, as it increases the level of life force energy or chi. Walking in nature, and connecting with the high vibrational frequencies contained in plants and trees, is wonderful for elevating your energies and enhancing your moods. Any exercise can alleviate stress, promote health and well-being, generally get you fit and help you feel better.

Decluttering

When I received my angel prayers one day while meditating, one in particular stuck me as a bit odd. I received a prayer on decluttering and letting go of possessions. Then I realised that there was a reason for this. Holding on to material things and possessions makes energy stuck and stagnate.

My grandmother was a classic example of someone who could not let go of possessions and who developed a hoarding habit. This, in essence, came from a sense of lack and of loss stemming back to her years during the Second World War in Britain when rationing was in place. She had also lost people who were close to her. She held on to things that were no use: old papers, magazines, books, knick-knacks, junk, food containers, clothes and shoes that no longer fit or were worn out, and food beyond its sell-by date. Things were stacked up in piles against her walls, and her cupboards were full to the brim. In many ways her hoarding was extremely wasteful. She would buy tins of food that she would not eat, and items from shops that she would never use.

The house became difficult to clean and manage. Eventually, one New Year's Day, she fell out of bed and was unable to free herself because she had become wedged between the bed and the pile of bedding and clothes piled up against the wall. After this incident (which could have been very dangerous) she agreed to start letting some of her stuff go. Her hoarding habit was unhealthy and was taken to the extreme, but it shows how clutter can take over someone's life.

Regularly let go of stuff you no longer want or need. Give items to charity that someone else can make use of and recycle as much as you can. I regularly put things in those charity donation bags you get through the letterbox and then put outside your door for collection when full.

Have a day dedicated to decluttering. Pick a room and start with just a drawer. When that drawer is done pick another drawer. When the room is done pick another room. One bit at a time is all that is needed, and you may be surprised at how much you get done.

Less clutter helps develop a cleaner, healthier and more energetic home. Excessive clutter can make you stressed and can also be distracting. By devoting some time to decluttering you can have a more positive and productive life and save time because you will know where everything is, and your home will be easier to keep clean and tidy.

Decluttering, however, doesn't just apply to material things. It applies to life as well. Meditation, for example, can help declutter your mind. Journaling can declutter your thoughts by putting them down on paper.

Reducing commitments can help streamline your life and raise your energy levels. Make a list of commitments you have during the course of the week and analyse them. Are there some that you could delegate to others in your family or workplace? Do you need to learn to say 'No'? Could you get up earlier to get certain things done? Then you would have more time to yourself doing the things you want to do. Do you need to organise your time more effectively and be more productive? Think also about the distractions you have. Constantly trawling through social media, watching TV programmes that don't give you joy or watching TV for the sake of it, playing endless hours of computer games instead of getting on with things... There's a whole list of mindless activities to distract you from getting things done.

When you engage in decluttering your life of not just physical things but also unnecessary activities you will probably find yourself happier, healthier, less stressed, and with more time on your hands. Your energies will be lifted and you will feel more in control.

Cord Cutting with Archangel Michael

This exercise is excellent for raising spiritual energies and for getting rid of attachments that weigh us down daily.

Cord cutting is an excellent way of removing the spiritual debris and attachments that we develop as we progress through life. These etheric cords develop with our interactions with people. These may be from relationships (business and personal), from friendships, and from acquaintances. Some may be positive interactions, some may be negative. Some ethereal cords can never be cut, such as those with our children.

Cord cutting can be useful in cleansing our aura if

there has been upset or hurt, or if there have been fear-based relationships. By cord cutting you are not harming the other person in any way or sending negative energies back to them. It is a form of releasing on an energetic level so that their energies cannot affect you in a negative way.

Michael is portrayed as holding a sword of light, with which he can lovingly cut the etheric cords of attachment that no longer serve our higher self. In doing this exercise Michael may cut cords that you are not aware of. I use this exercise regularly to keep my vibrational energies high.

Sit in a quiet place where you will not be disturbed. Visualise Archangel Michael standing in front of you with his sword of light. See if there are any cords that are attached to you that need removing and ask Archangel Michael to assist you in cutting these and any other etheric cords as needed. Visualise Archangel Michael removing the cords from your body. You may even see cords attached to you in unusual places.

Now visualise a bowl, a cauldron or any other vessel that contains a pure light. See the cords that have been severed placed into this vessel of light to be cleansed and transmuted. Now ask Archangel Michael to heal the areas from where the cords have been removed so that you and the other person or people are whole.

When you are ready, finish the exercise by taking a few breaths and seal and protect the aura above the head, below the feet and side to side at arm's length all around in love, light and peace. See yourself as fully healed and at peace.

Chapter 8

Connecting to Angels Through Meditation

Daily Meditation

When we begin to meditate we can discover a whole world within ourselves. Meditation can take us on a journey of wonder and of self-discovery to an inner world. It can help in quietening the mind and can help reduce irrelevant thoughts so that connection can be made with your highest spiritual aspect.

The practice of meditation can reduce stress, promote relaxation, help improve concentration, lower blood pressure, assist the body to heal itself, help reduce the development of stress-related diseases and illnesses and help develop spiritual growth.

Meditation assists in calming the mind and therefore allows clearer communication with the divine angelic beings. It can be likened to tuning into a specific radio station or frequency. Meditation helps to fine-tune the psyche to raise your energetic field and to access the finer spiritual realms more easily, in the same way that prayer assists in connecting with a higher consciousness. It focuses the mind, clears away negativity and stress and assists in giving you clear transmissions form the angelic realms and the divine consciousness.

The following is a simple meditation practice for you to use. Try to meditate regularly and make it part of your daily routine. It is better to meditate at a regular time. You may wish to do it in the morning or evening or both, once you become proficient at it. Remember that meditation is an acquired skill. Perseverance is key.

Find a suitable place where you can conduct your meditation without being disturbed. It is better, if you can, to have a place that you can use for your meditation. This can be a corner of a room or any space that you can make your own. This may be in a bedroom or a dining room or even a shed at the bottom of the garden. I'm lucky in that I have a small room. It's a space that no one else uses and it is a place where I can put my crystals, spiritual objects and pictures of angels.

When you start your meditation or any spiritual practice it is nice to record any feelings or experiences that you may have. Record these in a journal.

Simple Meditation Exercise

Find a quiet place where you will not be disturbed. Unplug the phone. Switch the mobile off. Sit comfortably upright in a chair, or in any other seated position that you find comfortable. Close your eyes and take a nice deep breath. Uncross your arms and legs and have your feet planted firmly on the floor. Perhaps you wish to sit cross-legged in a lotus position. Do whatever is most comfortable for you. Your spine should be straight and aligned.

Focus on your feet. Visualise roots sprouting from your feet, anchoring you to the earth and grounding you. Draw up through these roots the energy of the earth, which will empower you and help to clear away all negative energy and give you grounding.

Now begin to focus on your breath. Take a deep breath in. When you breathe out, imagine all the stresses and strains of the day melting away. Breathe in and feel that you are breathing in peace and relaxation. Breathe out and see all the tension and worries melt away.

As you continue to breathe in, imagine that you are breathing in a pure white light. As you breathe out, imagine you are breathing out a grey mist. The grey mist is all the tension, worry, problems and niggles you may have encountered during the day.

Once this is done, still your mind and focus just on the breath.

Sit in this peace for five or ten minutes. If your mind wanders, bring it back to focus on your breathing. Focus on your chest gently lifting up and down as you breathe. Focus on the beat of your heart as it pumps the blood around your body. Acknowledge any thoughts that arise and see them float away into the ether.

When you are done, feel at peace and fully relaxed.

At the end of your practice, surround yourself with a translucent bubble to help seal in the peace and to protect yourself from negative emotions. Be of joy and positivity and give thanks for the experience. See the bubble expand fifteen feet below you, fifteen feet above you and fifteen feet from each side of you and fill it with love, light and peace.

If you can, aim to meditate for around twenty minutes. But remember that even five minutes is better than no minutes. Try to do this practice daily. You will be amazed at the beneficial effect that meditating will have on your health and well-being. There will be times when you do this practice when your mind keeps wandering. This is normal, so don't be put off. Simplicity and perseverance are key. To stop and be still is the best foundation for any meditation practice.

Meditation and Connecting to Angels

Throughout the centuries mystics, healers, saints and enlightened souls have connected to the divine through the art of meditation. This may be done through repetition of prayers, mantras, connecting to nature, reading scripture or by sitting quietly and focusing on the breath. There are many different routes to the meditative state.

Ancient people connected to the inner world of angels and spirits through altered mind states, dance, drum beats, or retreating to distant caves for months or years at a time. In the modern, fast-paced world where we live this is not possible. We have houses to maintain, kids to take to school, the mother-in-law to visit, family to keep in touch with and work to do that pays our bills.

The practice of sitting quietly in meditation regularly can assist in making those inner connections to the ethereal world without having to delve into those ancient practices, which would be wonderful to experience but not achievable for most people. Sitting quietly and focusing on the breath are key to connecting to the universal consciousness that surrounds us. Meditation is a doorway to connecting to the angelic realms and to receiving the guidance and inner wisdom that we would not normally acquire in the fast-paced lives we live today.

Meditation is an important part of my daily practice. I meditate for at least twenty minutes daily, in the morning before I get ready for work or my day ahead. In the past I suffered from anxiety and low self-esteem, but daily meditation helped me regain my self-confidence and restore balance and harmony to my life. While that is good for me and fits in with my schedule, you will need to find your own routine to fit meditation practice into your own life. You may want to meditate in the evening when the kids have gone to bed, and you may not even be able to meditate for a full twenty minutes. Start doing little and often and continue to build on your practice to find what is right for you.

You do not need to live the life of a hermit to achieve

the calmness and well-being that meditation can bring. Meditation is, after all, an acquired skill that you need to persevere with.

Meditation is very useful in helping reverse the effects of stress, in addition to calming the mind and the emotions.

We live very full and often stressful lives. Continued stress can affect our bodies, our mood and our behaviour and can ultimately lead to many health problems. When under threat the adrenal glands release certain hormones so that the body can prepare for flight or fight. This in turn causes our muscles to tense, our blood pressure to increase – making our heart beat more quickly – and our breathing to become faster and shallower. At many points in my life I had quite severe panic attacks. This was in part my body's reaction to stress (part of my own fight or flight response). This response is part of our ancestral make-up and has been in humans since the time when we had to run from wild animals or faced real danger. In today's life some people find that this response is provoked not only at times of real danger but also when they are faced with what they perceive as stressful situations.

During meditation the brainwaves alter to a distinctive alpha pattern. While meditating one can experience enhanced mental awareness while simultaneously feeling deep relaxation.

People who regularly meditate can move into this mode at will. This allows them to counter stress more efficiently and helps lower the blood pressure and combat muscle pain. Regular meditation can help develop spiritual and psychic abilities in addition to assisting in calming our mind and emotions. It also is excellent for relieving stress.

Stress creates a fog over our mind so that we cannot see or perceive situations with clarity, and it clouds our judgement. Meditation helps to lift this fog so that we can see situations as they really are and react to them in a more calm and positive manner.

When your mind and body are calm you can access your intuition and your imagination. This is where your hopes, dreams and creativity come from. When you can access this source of creativity and wisdom you will find that you will be able to attract what you want in life more easily. You will also be clearer about what you want to attract and want to create in your life.

Preparing Your Space

Once you have chosen a space in which to meditate you may wish to prepare it in such a way that it enhances your meditation experience. Whether it is a spare room that you can claim for yourself or simply a small space within an area that you can call your own, it is nice to prepare it in such a way that it reflects your spiritual practice.

Cleanse

Cleanse your space both physically and energetically. Keep it clean, tidy and free from dust. Cleanse your space energetically by using a sage smudge stick or a singing bowl or some tingshas. Smudge sticks can be bought from any good New Age store. Light one end of the stick and place it on an abalone shell or, if you don't have one, on a plate to catch the embers. Waft the smoke with a feather fan or simply your hand. Set the intention as you waft the smoke that you are clearing the space of any negative energies. Extinguish the smudge stick when you are done. Smudging is likened to having an energetic shower and will get rid of negativity. Crystals or other objects can be cleansed by passing them through the sage smoke to clear away negative debris.

Alternatively you can sound a singing bowl, which is a metal bowl that makes a distinct sound when rubbed along the rim by a rounded wooden mallet. Or you can ring a pair of tingshas. These are small Tibetan cymbals that make a ringing sound when struck together. Any of these can be used to energetically clear the space around your dedicated meditation area. These tools can also be used to clear negative energies in any rooms or areas in your home.

Arguments, violent games (or films) or any negative behaviour can leave an imprint in the environment. By smudging or using sound, any negative debris in the environment can be energetically brushed away to leave an uplifted energy.

Furnishing Your Space

The following items are suggestions regarding what you may wish to put in your meditation space.

- You may have a table or shelf to put objects on. You may have a cupboard to place items in, which can be opened when meditation practice takes place.
- A nice chair, cushions or a beanbag to sit on.
- Items to inspire, statues, pictures, etc.
- Nice covers and soft furnishings.
- A touch of nature, such as a plant or flowers.
- Crystals, special stones, feathers, etc.
- Aromas, such as essential oils in a burner and incense.
- Candles.

Meditation Summary

Try to meditate daily. Find a time that is suitable to you. You may prefer meditating in the morning, as I do, or in the evening when the kids are in bed. Try to do at least ten minutes a day, and ideally twenty minutes daily. Sit in a comfortable position in a chair, and make sure your feet are connected to the floor. If you are short (like me) put a cushion or something similar under your feet. Sit with your back straight. If you're agile enough you can sit on the floor cross-legged, like a yogi. You can always lie down, but be careful not to fall asleep. Always remember to see the roots developing from your feet, grounding you. Record your experiences and how your meditation makes you feel in a journal.

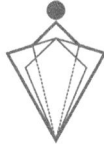

Chapter 9

Angel Prayers and Angel Altars

When I was younger I said my prayers regularly. A relative gave me a copy of the Book of Common Prayer and, although I didn't understand some of it, each night I would look at it and read some of the prayers contained within. As I grew older I stopped saying prayers, but as I've got older still I've gone back to them. However, I believe that you can make your own prayers as well as following the more common ones of faith.

Over the years I've found my belief again in the power of prayer and I do absolutely believe that prayers work. I liken prayer to putting the power of positive intention into the universe and that the universe will respond accordingly. Prayers are requests to the higher source, the universal consciousness, or God – however you wish to see it – and they are clear statements of what you need assistance with or guidance about. They are also excellent ways to connect with the angels that are there to help and assist you on your life's journey. According to scripture, that's what angels are there for: to take your prayers up to the heavens so that God answers them. Whenever you are in times of need it is comforting to take time in taking to the act of prayer and asserting to yourself that your prayers will be answered in one way or another.

When you offer prayer it is a request of positive intent to that higher source to resolve your issue for the highest good. It's about giving your problems to a higher spiritual energy that has the ability and the knowledge to resolve the problems and issues that exist. It is about faith and about trust and accessing that deep inner knowing of your own that your prayers will be answered. It is not something that can be tested by science. However, there are many examples out there where people have had their prayers answered, sometimes in miraculous ways. I belong to a prayer group online, where members will request prayers to be said on their behalf for various troubles. There have been some amazing results, and some have been quite miraculous. Requests for healing have been realised, disputes have been resolved positively, gravely ill people have been healed and negative situations have been turned into positive ones. These are some examples from among the many other prayers that have been answered.

There is a saying that prayer is likened to talking to God, whereas meditation is listening.

There are many different ways of offering prayers throughout the various religions and belief systems.

Prayer can take the form of the act of formal prayer, by using a rosary, by saying mantras, by sitting quietly in meditation or by taking part in a ritual. In addition to this you have the option of praying on your own or with others.

What better way of praying than having an altar as a focus for your prayers and meditation, and as a focus point for your connection with the angelic realm? Altars are not created to worship angels, but are used merely as a focus point for you to reflect with positive intention.

My angels guided me to the items needed for my altar, and they can do the same for you. Decide where you want to make a dedicated space. It can be in your bedroom or in any quiet space in your home. It can even be a space under the stairs. Ask the angels to guide you to make a space and find the items you need for your altar.

I was guided to make an angel table and had seen a picture of an angel ornament in a book that I had recently bought. I walked in a shop and saw the exact same one. Quickly, I snatched it up and took it to the counter. I explained to the shop owner that I had seen the same ornament in a book, but she insisted that I couldn't have as they were new items in the shop. I needed some gold cloth for my table, and I was guided to a nearby market stall. There, unbelievably, were some gold cloth offcuts being sold very cheaply. Lastly, I needed a gold candle. Again, I was guided to visit a shop at the other side of town that I hadn't been in for years. I walked in, looked at the shelf, and there was one solitary gold church-style candle.

I got home and made my angel table. A day later I decided to go into the attic to find a book. I pushed open the attic lid, tentatively climbed the stepladder and peered through the opening. There, right on the edge of the opening and directly in my eyeline was a small gold and white angel made of cloth, like the sort that would be hung on a Christmas tree. I was stunned. I had never seen it before. It didn't belong to me. Many times both my husband and I had been up into the attic space and there had been no angel to be seen. To this day I don't know where it came from. Shaking with disbelief, I picked the little angel up and placed her on my angel table. She has been there ever since. I truly believe it was a sign from the angels to remind me that they were around.

The angels have been a huge part of my life ever since. I speak to my angels most days and they have appeared to me many times. I was even guided to go back to my old, less stressful job. They have totally changed my life for the better and they can do the same for you.

Making an Angel Altar

An angel altar can become a place for spiritual enlightenment, a place to connect to your angels and to gain insight into life. It can be a place where you let go of stresses and strains and put perspective into situations, revealing valuable insight. It can be a place of serenity, harmony, balance and, above all, a place where you can find peace.

An altar in your home is a place to reflect, a refuge for you to enjoy and be peaceful in, a place that gives spiritual sustenance.

The altar can be set up on a shelf or on top of a chest of drawers. You can have more than one altar if you wish. Place the altar where you can see it and where you can spend time in quiet reflection. Have a comfy chair you can sit on. If the altar is in the bedroom you may just wish to use the bed as a seat. Decorate your altar with a beautiful cloth. I like to choose a plain cloth in gold or white – something simple. Keep your altar clean and free from dust.

Pictures and statues of angels will give inspiration and act as a portal to connect with the angels. You may wish to have a display of cut flowers on your altar to add life, scent and beauty to your table. Be sure, though, to remove flowers that are dead and not to make your altar too cluttered.

Place a candle on your altar to light each time you spend time connecting and meditating. You can also use incense or aromatherapy oils in a burner to create beautiful aromas (make sure any candles or incense burn safely, and never leave flames unattended). You can use a different coloured candle to connect with each different angel, or just use a white candle. Candles symbolise spiritual light, bringing light to darkness, illumination, and revealing truths. Candles are good to use as part of a focus meditation. Light a candle and focus on the flame as all other thoughts or worries melt away.

Crystals, flowers, shells, bells and feathers make pretty additions to your altar, as well as pictures and photos. Angel ornaments and angel images are easily bought and can be used on your altar. Make your altar as appealing as you can. This is your space to connect. When you have finished, dedicate your space to the angels and invite them in. Ask them to bless your altar and know that anytime you wish to connect with the angels you can spend time with them in your sacred space.

Angel Prayers

These prayers came to me during the summer of 2015. I have used them to great effect at various times, and they are put here for personal use. They are prayers so that the angels may guide us and help us with the challenges that we may face in life. They give thanks for the blessings in our lives, and they are requests for help with anything that makes us feel stuck and for healing purposes. These prayers were originally published in my first book, *Walking into the Light*.

Morning Prayer to St Michael

I give thanks for the day ahead
And ask St Michael to protect me at all times,
To surround my being with a bubble of love and light,
So that I may shine,
And repel all negativity
That I may encounter
And to fill my day with happiness and joy,
So it is.
Thank you.

Prayer to Quan Yin

I ask Quan Yin and the angels of the violet flame
To colour my path with violet,
To protect me in my travels today,
So that everything goes well today
And every day,

According to divine order,
So it is.
Thank you.

Evening Prayer to the Angels

I give thanks for all I have experienced today,
For all the people I have encountered,
And I ask to let go of all troubles and worries,
So that I may sleep soundly
And be restful,
And wake up ready for the new day,
Full of positive intent,
So it is.
Thank you.

For Decluttering

I ask Archangel Michael and his legion of angel
helpers
To assist me in decluttering my mind and my
home,
So that I may progress with ease and flow,
To have more energy and space,
In my physical and mental realms,
So that I may be at one
With my mind, home and well-being,
And able to invite positive energies and
experiences,
So it is.
Thank you.

For Healing

I ask Archangels Michael and Raphael
To assist in this powerful healing,
To remove all pain, fear and suffering,
To place (*name*) on the road to recovery,
To give courage, strength and peace,
And well-being,
For the highest good of all,
So it is.
Thank you.

Removing Negativity

I ask Quan Yin and the angels of the violet flame
To transmute all negative energies,
Surrounding (*name*),
Leaving only positive, peaceful and loving
experiences,
For the highest good of all,
So it is.
Thank you.

For Relationships

I ask Archangel Michael and his legions of light
To transmute any negativity,
And restore my relationships,
With balance, harmony, peace and love,
So that I may be free from fear and harm,
And request that Archangel Michael
Uses his sword of truth,
To cut ties with all that no longer serves,
For my highest good,

So it is.
Thank you.

For Abundance

I ask Archangel Ariel and her fairy realm
To lavish me with abundance,
So that I may be free
To express myself fully,
In love and joy,
And have enough to share.
I give thanks for these wondrous gifts,
And know that it is for my highest good,
And for those around me,
So it is
Thank you.

Connecting with the Angels with Candles

The following is extracted from my book *Walking into the Light: A Seeker's Guide to Spiritual Development* (2018).

In meditation it is nice to light a candle. I find that lighting a candle with the intention of connecting with angels is a wonderful way to connect more deeply with their loving presence, while also enhancing and deepening the practice of meditation.

The use of candles has a practical purpose, in that they give a natural form of light. They also have a spiritual significance too. Go into many places of worship and you will see candles used in ceremonies. They represent symbolically the light of Christ in the Christian Church. Many religious ceremonies use candles of a significant number, which are lit at certain times during or before rituals. The use of candles in ceremonies is an ancient practice.

Angels can be contacted at any time, but I feel there is a certain sort of magic in lighting a candle that is of the colour associated with a specific angel. Traditionally beeswax candles would be used, as they are more natural. However, you can use any good-quality candle that can be purchased from any good New Age store. Make sure that before you light your candle you have a sturdy holder to put it in, and that the candle is not going to fall over.

If you wish, candles can be dressed before using. I

personally like to use essential oils, as they add aroma to the candles. The act of applying an oil to the candle adds your personal energy to it. Before lighting the candle, however, use visualisation to remove any negative energies from the candle. Set the intent that the lighting of the candle is a representation of the light of the angels, illuminating your connection to these divine beings.

The following table has a list of candle colours that can be used with a particular archangel. These colours are not set in stone. If a different colour for that archangel resonates for you then use that colour. These candle colours and associations came to me as a result of my meditating on each angel and candle colour. You may find something different.

When working with the angels and candles, as with all spiritual working, intent is the key. Hold a peaceful space and a pure heart for your spiritual practice. You may wish to say a small prayer beforehand. It doesn't have to be anything complicated. When you are finished, blow the candle out. If you wish the candle to burn out by itself choose small candles to work with, which take less time to burn down and are therefore safer. Never leave a flame unattended.

White	Red	Yellow
Azrael	Gabriel	Jophiel
Metatron	Michael	Sandaphon
Zadkiel	Metatron	Uriel
		Zadkiel

Pink	Green	Purple
Chamuel	Ariel	Michael
Jeremiel	Raphael	Raziel
Jophiel		

Orange	Blue	Silver
Gabriel	Michael	Haniel
Raguel	Raphael	

Select the colour of candle and the name of the angel you wish to work with. Light the candle with the intention of connecting with the angel. You may wish to burn some incense or oils in a burner as well.

Sit comfortably, and take a few deep breaths. Draw down the white light, a pure crystalline light, through the top of your head. Now visualise your aura expanding outwards as you ask for this connection to be made with your chosen angel. Focus on the candle flame as you connect. You may wish to say the name of the angel.

As you connect you may feel tickles on your face, a change in the air and a change in the energy of the room. You should always feel uplifted. If the energy feels heavy ask it to go away, and request that only beings of the pure light of God or of the divine source may enter your space. When you feel you have the connection, be aware of any impressions, images or words you may have. Notice how it feels. Stay with it for as long as you feel comfortable. If you drift off, bring your focus back to the breath. Once you have finished, give thanks for your connection. Now write what you have experienced and how it felt in your journal.

Asking the Angels for Protection

Whenever you feel the need for protection, ask your angels to be at your side. Remember that the angels can be anywhere at any time, so you will not be taking them away from any important mission. Although the angels are always by your side you can actively ask them to protect you, particularly if you are travelling, visiting unfamiliar areas or feel unsafe. Knowing that the angels are there by your side can give you reassurance and help you feel protected. You may feel your angels close by, giving comfort and keeping you safe. You can ask them to help you if you are nervous, perhaps if you are at an important meeting or interview.

Don't be afraid to ask the angels to intervene in situations of conflict or difficulty. You'd be amazed how the angels can come in and help resolve situations with positive outcomes or generally ease difficult situations. You can ask the angels to smooth your path in readiness for the day ahead to ensure that things go well. You can ask the angels to protect your home, and you can visualise an angel guarding all four corners of your house or living space.

Inevitably situations may arise that are out of your control. But always know that the angels are by your side, looking after your best interests.

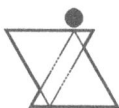

Chapter 10

Giving an Angel Reading

Giving an angel card reading is very different from giving any other type of reading. For me it's much more loving, guiding and positive in delivery.

You don't have to be a trained medium to give accurate readings. It is better, though, to work on your intuition, on raising your vibration and on developing psychically. There are many classes available where you can develop your psychic and mediumship abilities. I attended classes for a number of years to fine-tune my abilities and to open up to the world of spirit. The more you practise giving readings the better you will get. Conduct your readings with an open heart, ask for guidance from the angelic kingdom and always give your best.

When I first started doing readings using tarot cards many years ago, I found it very difficult to connect with the cards and felt uncomfortable using them. In fact this stopped me giving readings for some time. Since then I have moved on to angel oracle cards.

There are many to choose from. I have over a dozen different sets, including quite a few from Doreen Virtue*, who has contributed some beautiful sets of cards over the years.

Cleanse your cards energetically initially by praying over them, knocking them with your knuckles or passing them through the smoke from a smudge stick. Then get to know your cards before using them. Touch each card to infuse it with your energy. Look at each card. What does the symbolism on the card say to you? You may wish to sleep with the cards. Place them under your pillow at night to infuse the cards with your energy.

Readings, for me, should be inspiring, supporting, and given with love and grace. They should be uplifting with an insightfulness that can help the sitter resolve any issues they have in a positive manner. A reading should shed light on matters and assist the sitter in understanding how they can move forward.

There are various ways of giving readings, and many different thoughts and practices on how to give readings. An important rule of thumb that I learnt when I was taught how to read was not to tell the sitter about anything that could not be changed. If you psychically 'see' that there is an impending death you do not tell the sitter. Telling them will not change the event and will cause them endless worry and stress. It's just not constructive. If, however, you can see that a danger can be averted, such as brakes failing on a car, then give the sitter warning as it averts any crisis. It may not necessarily stop the incident happening, but the sitter can be vigilant to any mishaps that may occur in the future. Warning the sitter to be vigilant is empowering, as it potentially averts any crisis. My husband was told over thirty years ago by a psychic that he would die upside down. This has stuck with him ever since, and was a completely irresponsible and horrible thing to say to him.

Readings

When giving a reading for someone, occasionally the information brought forward might not make sense for the person. Don't let this dint your confidence. Sometimes the information given in a reading can be for months or sometimes years ahead. This has been a personal experience of mine. I've had readings that were a few years ahead which are only coming to fruition now. At the time they didn't make sense to me. Sometimes information is brought forward by spirit that is relevant for that person at that time but that will only make sense later.

Also, because of our free will choices, certain events in the future may change or be delayed. Likewise, certain events may not be revealed to the person you are reading for, as that person may have to go through specific life events to progress spiritually. For example, I conducted a reading for someone I knew very well. At the end of the reading she told me that it was accurate but she was surprised that I didn't pick up that she was to change her occupation. As it was, she did change her occupation but went through a series of challenging events. I believe she had to go through those experiences and hence they were not revealed in the reading. As it is now, her life has greatly improved and those experiences took her on a path that neither of us could have ever envisioned.

Sometimes information can be interpreted inaccurately when the reader's mind comes in and tries to make sense of the information being given rather than just saying it as it is revealed. Even though it doesn't make sense to you, the reader, it may make perfect sense for the person you are reading for. Don't let logic dictate your reading. Trust and go with the flow. Don't wrestle with it.

When giving a reading it's good to be prepared. Sometimes readings may happen spontaneously, and that's good too. But, to give a good and professional reading, it's always wise to prepare and to give the best experience for your sitter that you can.

Clarity of Thought

It seems obvious, but having a late night out and overindulging the night before giving a reading the next day doesn't help you give your best. Be free of toxins, choose your food carefully, drink plenty of water and have an early night, so that the next day you are feeling refreshed. Meditation will also help clear the mind. While meditating you can request that the angels help you give an accurate reading. You can also tune into the sitter prior to the appointment.

Clear the Space

Clear and tidy any clutter. Cover the area or table you will be working on with a nice cloth. It could be a nice piece of material you have bought cheaply at the local market or a specific altar or reading cloth bought at a specialist store. On your table you could place a nice statue, perhaps of an angel, a crystal ball, crystals to help you focus or a small display of flowers. You are working energetically when you give a reading, so have your space work for you with items that enhance and lift the special energy. You may wish to hold a crystal in your non-dominant hand while giving the reading. This will assist in giving you a focus in addition to the cards and will help in raising your vibrational energy.

Cleanse the Cards

Hold the cards in your hands and see yourself connecting with them. Visualise a white light all around your cards, which will remove any negative energies. You may wish to say a prayer. Call in angelic guidance. Some people like to knock their cards to remove any energetic residue by tapping their cards with their knuckles. It's all down to preference, so do what feels right to you.

Connect

When you give your reading visualise the sitter's and your energies connecting. Shuffle the cards to put your energy on to them. You may wish your reader to shuffle the cards too. Some readers ask the sitter to place their hands on the cards, then the reader will place their hands over the top to establish an energetic connection. Some readers let the sitter choose the cards, and sometimes the reader chooses them. Choose which method is best for you. Use your intuition. Connect with your guides and ask that you give the best reading possible. Connect with your cards and ask for angelic guidance and protection. Keep your energies high while reading. If you feel them dip or you feel as if you've lost connection, consciously raise the vibrations and reconnect with your guidance.

Card Layouts

There are many different layouts you can use when consulting the cards. Some people (such as me) like to read in straight lines. If you are doing a quick reading for yourself you may have a specific question in mind and you may pick a card to give an answer to the situation. A simple reading to get you going can be to choose three cards: past, present and future. For a more in-depth reading you may choose twelve cards, one for each month of the year. Another common card layout is the Celtic Cross spread. This is the layout recommended in many oracle card sets. I prefer to lay my cards out in straight lines as I like my reading to flow rather than get too bogged down with specific layouts. If cards jump out while shuffling I will put them to one side, as they can give further insight at the end of the reading. I don't limit myself to one set. I may use one main set, then another set to pick a couple of cards for an overview to tie up the reading.

Conclusion

Once you feel you have reached the end of the session conclude the reading. Give a general overview of what has been said and ask your sitter if they have any questions or if there is anything that they didn't understand. If there are any issues that have arisen during the session or it has been a challenging reading, ask the angels to intervene and give healing to the situation. After the reading, take time to visualise and cut any etheric cords between you and the sitter.

Checklist to summarise the points given
- Clarity of thought
- Clear the space
- Cleanse the cards
- Connect
- Card Layout
- Conclusion.

Fears

Confronting our fears and overcoming them is an essential part of walking the spiritual path. It takes courage to live spiritually, and fear may be an element or an emotion that you need to overcome. This could be the fear of the unknown, a fear of what people will think, a fear how things will progress in the future or a fear of change.

When connecting with the angels the movement of energy within the subtle body may take the individual by surprise. You should not be fearful of this movement of energy, but rather move through the experience with feelings of love, acceptance and gratitude. By embracing the experience as it unfolds the fear will move to one side. Holding positive intentions is key to the experience. If you intend to connect to higher angelic guidance, which is of pure light and loving energy, there is no room for fear.

My initial experience in connecting with the angelic realms was one of awe and wonder. I wanted to hold on to the feeling of bliss and love as it moved into my subtle body or aura. I literally felt as though I was on cloud nine, such was the encounter.

Fear is usually the resistance that is felt when experiencing something that is new and unknown. So let go of fear, assert that all is well and of love and of peace, and move through it.

If something really does not feel right, or is not of love or of peace, then assert to yourself that it leaves immediately.

Dealing with fear is a part of the spiritual journey. We must learn to walk through all fear and turn that fear into focused awareness.

*NOTE: Since writing this chapter Doreen Virtue has been in the process of removing her name from her oracle cards, but there are many other beautiful decks out there by other authors.

Chapter 11

Channelling Through Writing

This is by far one of my favourite methods of working with spirit guides and angels. A lot of writing that I have done doesn't come from me, my ego self. It comes from a higher source. At times I have written passages that are hugely profound, and not something that I would have written myself. Sometimes, when I sit to do automatic writing, it just doesn't happen, and that's OK too. Automatic writing can be done using a pen and paper or it can be done using a keyboard. This choice is entirely yours.

When you channel messages through automatic writing it gives you the opportunity to draw through information from a higher source. It can open doorways to contact higher spiritual beings, such as angels, archangels, guardian angels, spirit guides, ascended masters and beyond. It can also give you the opportunity to channel information from deceased individuals who were once masters in their field, such as the arts, poetry, literature, spirituality and so on.

The scope is limitless. The only things that limit your potential in this field are you and your ego.

When you start to channel you may decide that it's you making it up, it's silly or that you can't do it. The way to get around this is to tune in and just start writing, even if at first it doesn't seem to make sense. Try not to let your logical mind take over. It will get easier the more you practise. You are not working with the thinking part of your mind. You are working with the intuitive and creative part of your mind. To do it successfully you need to put your mind to one side and allow the words to flow.

Getting in the Zone

It is best to practise automatic writing in a quiet place where you won't be disturbed. You can set the scene if you wish by lighting a candle, burning incense or playing relaxing music in the background. You may even prefer complete silence and stillness. That's OK too. Do whatever is best for you.

Sitting quietly in a meditative state is the best way to get your mind quiet and free from chatter by putting your thinking mind to one side. At this point you can call in your guides and angels to assist you in your task. Call upon energies that are of 100 per cent light – the highest guidance you can access. Align yourself to your heart centre and surround yourself in positive energies. You can call upon Archangel Michael for protection and guidance as you write.

The tools you use to write with are entirely up to

you. You may wish to use a computer and a keyboard or pens and paper. I prefer the latter. I have a specific pad for the purpose and use gel pens, as they flow more freely. Scratchy pens inhibit the flow.

To begin with you may wish to write down the intent that you intend to channel, or a question that you wish to have answered.

Begin to write down any impressions you may get. The first few sentences may seem like gobbledygook, but stick with it. Don't try to analyse it. Just go with the flow and write whatever comes through. Record what you get, even if you think it's just your imagination.

When you start to write you may notice that the words that come through are very different from your own. They may be quite old-fashioned in context or words that you don't normally use, or it may be that your sentences are written in a different way from how you would normally write. You may also notice, if you're using a pen, that your handwriting changes. Don't read through what you have got until you feel that you have finished. You will naturally know when you have come to the end of your session. You may feel the energy subside and feel that what you have written is sufficient.

When you have completed your session, give thanks. You can say it out loud or write it down. Giving gratitude shows appreciation and, I feel, strengthens the communication for next time. It's good to complete these tasks with love and appreciation in your heart.

In some sessions you will feel the connection very strongly, an energy that sweeps through you. You may feel your hand being 'taken over'. You may just receive impressions or hear the words as you write. You may feel different sensations and have different experiences each time you sit to do this exercise. Sometimes it will come easily, other times not so easily. Don't worry if sometimes you don't get that connection or it doesn't seem to flow. Some sessions are like that. Some days you will get a lot, some days very little.

Take time to read through what you have written. Periodically read through your writings, as there may be insights that you received that you have forgotten about, or you may see a pattern to your writing. You may also receive profound information that is significant to you or that you may wish to share with others.

Try to complete your practice regularly and have a special place to do it in. With frequent practice, say once a week, you will find that your skills will develop and the process will become easier.

Chapter 12

Angels on the Go

Angels are excellent companions to call upon when you are on the go, when out and about – whether it is going on a journey, working, socialising or whenever there is emotional upset, conflict or strife. They can be called upon to assist in all areas of your life.

When you call upon the angels to help you in any way you are not taking them away from more important tasks. They are constantly available and can be in many places simultaneously. They are not physical beings, but spiritual ones.

Angels are beings of light that are here to assist us in our earthly life. They are beings of love and are here to help us in whatever way possible to make our lives peaceful, loving and joyful. They are there to guide and comfort us and are there to help if we ask them to. I don't feel that it is selfish to ask for their assistance, even if those things may seem trivial, but I certainly don't think that they would assist us in doing something that we shouldn't do, nor help in exerting our influence over another person or being. They are there to make our lives as joyful as possible and they can only give assistance that is for our highest good. Sometimes when you request the help of the angels the results may be something that you did not anticipate.

The angels can be asked for things that will be of benefit to our highest nature. We can ask for things that make our lives happy and peaceful, for things that are for the good of ourselves and others. Angels cannot be summoned to do anything that is not at one with good or with God's light. They act as God's helpers and messengers. Angels act on God's behalf by bringing peace to the world, and this is their divine mission. When we live our life in a more peaceful way we are more in tune with our authentic self.

When asking for the angels' help be specific in what you want help with, and then allow the angels to do their work and use their magic to give what is needed at that time. They symbolise purity and peace and can be looked upon to assist in times when things are out of balance, unsettled, or causing grief, worry or fear.

The angels can help with all situations, and they will help to attain the highest good for you and for others. All you need to do is ask, and they can be there to give emotional support and assistance in any circumstances.

The following are some examples of when you can call on the angels to help. The words you choose are not important, but the sincerity with which you ask is.

Car Parking Angel

A favourite example of mine of when the angels can come to the rescue in what could potentially be a stressful situation is that of finding a car parking space. Again, when you ask for assistance in this way, you are not taking the angels away from any important mission. I used the assistance from the angelic realm in this way many times before taking my invalid mother-in-law out shopping, and I was always guided to a perfect parking spot on the busiest of days in the small town where we live. I have also used angelic guidance when I have got lost when driving. An example of this was when I once had to travel to Manchester and I had no satellite navigation system. I took a wrong exit off the motorway and knew I was lost. I stopped by the side of the road and asked the angels to guide me on my way. As if by a miracle I had an inner knowledge of where to go, and lo and behold I got there with time to spare. My request of help from the angels was answered.

Colouring Your Path

This is a technique that I like to use before a busy and potentially stressful day. This can be done while meditating or in a quiet state before starting your day. Sit quietly, take a few deep breaths and still the mind. Bring your attention to the day ahead and the tasks that need to be completed. You can visualise a straight road ahead of you as you do this. Request Quan Yin and the angels of the violet flame to colour your path violet, to smooth the path ahead and the day's journey and activities. Ask the angels to ease your way through the day and ensure that the day goes well and smoothly. When you have finished, gives thanks for the angels' assistance. You can request the assistance of any archangel to help with your day ahead, of any archangel that resonates with you the most.

Resolving Conflict

If you find yourself in any conflict you can immediately request that the angels assist in resolving the situation. I've done this many times, namely once at work where there was a misunderstanding and I ended up in a potentially difficult situation. I have found that Archangel Michael is good for resolving conflict. In this instance I requested his help. The situation was immediately defused, and peace was restored in an instant.

When You are Nervous

If you have an important meeting, a job interview, a speech to make or any situation that causes you anxiety or to be nervous, call on your angels to help. This can be done in the morning, in a similar way to colouring your path for the day ahead, or it can be done in an instant by requesting the assistance of the angels to quell your nerves. Or it can be done by using both techniques. Sit in quiet contemplation while sending out positive vibes for the situation and enlisting the assistance of the angelic realm. If you still feel nervous, request the immediate assistance of the angels at that moment to help you.

Help with Relationships

If you are struggling with issues in relationships, ask the angels for assistance and divine guidance. Again, this can be done in any of the ways stated above, by making a request during a meditation, or by requesting immediate assistance if you suddenly find yourself in a difficult situation.

Another way of resolving issues in relationships is to call upon your guardian angel to speak to the other person's guardian angel. The words you choose are not important, but you must have love and sincerity in your heart for the resolution of whichever situation you wish to be resolved. Ask for guidance and assistance from the angels. Remember that you can't interfere with another person's free will and the angels cannot force things on another person on your behalf. It is up to the other person to respond how they wish to.

Sit in a quiet place, take a few deep breaths, and still the mind. Request that your guardian angel speaks to the other person's guardian angel on your behalf. Do not tell the angels how to resolve the situation. Just ask that it is resolved for the highest good of all involved. Trust in the angels to do their work on your behalf. Thank the angels when you are done.

Writing a Letter to Your Angels

This is another good way of resolving any situation that you are struggling with. Sit quietly with a pen and a piece of paper. Write down all that is troubling you on the paper. Make a request that the angels help you solve your problems, worries or concerns in the best way possible for the highest good. Once you have finished you can either put this letter into a box for the angels to work their magic or you can burn it and send it out the universe for the angels to work their magic (if you burn the paper do so safely, and use a fireproof container to catch the embers).

Ask Archangel Michael to Fix Things

Archangel Michael is brilliant at fixing things. Just ask. I've requested him many times to fix mechanical things, and many times they have been fixed as if by a miracle. If he can't fix them he will send along the right person for the job. Just ask and trust. Words are not important, just the sincerity of the request.

Blessing Others on Their Way

Just before writing this chapter I had a timely reminder from my angels that when we see people in strife or in despair we should request that the angels give blessings to help them as they go on their way.

Earlier today I was driving on my way home after picking up some dinner. I saw a man staggering across the road, very obviously high on drugs and talking to himself as he walked. At first, like many would do, I immediately judged him. How did he get in that state? Why did he allow himself to get like that?

The angels reminded me that when we see someone we should not judge them as we don't know their story, how they came to be like that or what tragedy or pain they have had in their lives to lead them to that point. So I blessed him on his way and asked the angels to help him. Giving blessing to others can be extended not just to family and friends but to people we see on the street, to strangers, and ultimately to people who don't even know that we have extended blessings on their behalf. It is done silently. I like to say in my head, 'Bless them on their way.' People can also be blessed in silent prayer. It's up to the individual whether they accept it or not, even when they don't know that that blessing has been extended to them. It's like giving blessings out to the universe and them landing on whoever is ready to receive them. It's a projection of love on to others: asking the angels and ultimately God's universal love to help and guide them along their way, whatever their circumstances.

Chapter 13

Stories of Angelic Encounters

Angel Encounters

There are multitudes of stories of the appearance of angels in the Bible. There are also some very famous examples of angelic visitors throughout history. Visions of angels are now being captured on CCTV, on video and on cameras everywhere. You only need to go online to find videos and photographs that give evidence to mysterious beings captured on film. Many of these are open to scepticism and there is great debate about their authenticity. However, some of the images captured are very difficult to explain rationally.

Angelic visions and apparitions through time have given hope and inspiration to many. Some stories follow of angelic intervention and visions, some of which have been greatly debated over time (and the legitimacy of some of the stories questioned). These stories, however, give insight into how the angels can impact on the lives of the believers, the experiences that people have had with angels and how these beings have given courage and faith to many. There is a whole host of stories in the media and throughout history. Only a few are included here. Some may be new to you. I've also included a little about John of God, a psychic healer who has performed many miraculous healings. Although he isn't specifically associated with angels he channels many entities, including saints, and he states that his healing comes directly from God.

Joan of Arc

Joan of Arc famously heard angelic voices speaking to her. She was known as the Maid of Orleans, was a French heroine, and was made a saint by the Roman Catholic Church. Her first encounter with who she believed was Archangel Michael was at the tender age of thirteen. She believed that she was guided by Archangel Michael, Archangel Gabriel, Saint Catherine and Saint Margaret. The female saints guided her with instructions on how to live her life until she was seventeen.

Later, Archangel Michael came through strongly to her with instructions to go to speak to the dauphin (the son of the king) of France, Charles VII. She was instructed that she was to help drive the English from French territories. This was during the latter stages of the Hundred Years War (1337–1453), which was a series of conflicts between the English and French kingdoms over who should rule France.

Charles's armies at the time were losing a war against the English for control of the country. When his generals turned her away the voices became more insistent. When Charles did eventually agree to meet Joan, the voices gave her signs to give him that indicated to him that she was undoubtedly receiving heavenly guidance. Joan went to lead the French armies in battle while carrying an ancient sword that the voices had guided her to find. Before going into battle she had a number of visions, which all came to pass. In her visions God directed her to take back her homeland from the English. In 1430 she was captured and given to the English, after which she was tried. The trial took place at Rouen, Normandy and was overseen by the English-backed church court. The proceedings, led by Bishop Pierre Cauchon and his advisors began on the morning of 21 February 1431. She was burnt at the stake for heresy and so did not live to see her vision coming to fruition: of the French winning back Paris from the English. She perished on 31 May 1431 at the age of just nineteen. Her remains were tossed into the Seine. She was canonised in 1920.

The Mons Angels

The appearance of angels on the battlefield during World War One has been much debated over the years. In August 1914 stories circulated about angels and saints having appeared on the battlefield to help Allied soldiers as they were retreating from Mons in Belgium. As the British and French soldiers were driven back by the Germans, many troops reported angelic and saintly visions.

One group of soldiers charged out of their trench towards the Germans. As the soldiers ran, an officer became aware of a large group of ghostly men with bows and arrows moving with him, leading the officer and his men towards the enemy trenches. It is said that the ghosts of the archers came to the aid of the British soldiers by firing their arrows against the opposing German troops. German prisoners claimed to have seen the phantom archers led by a mysterious figure on a white horse. Some believed the mysterious figure to be Saint George.

On another occasion on the battlefield, a lance corporal who had been injured claimed that his soldiers had observed three shining figures with faces that hovered above them in the sky. They watched the beings for half an hour. One of the figures was described as having outstretched wings. The corporal's army battalion had been beaten back after an attack by the Germans when the figures appeared. The corporal said that they were hovering over the German line, facing the British soldiers, and described them as having golden-coloured long, loose clothing. The vision gave the corporal and his soldiers hope.

There has been debate about whether these events actually happened or not. However, only the men who were on the battlefield at that time know whether or not they did.

Our Lady of Guadalupe

Juan Diego, a Mexican peasant and farmer aged fifty-seven, was making his way to Mass early on the morning of 9 December 1531. He lived with his elderly uncle, because his wife had died two years earlier.

While walking to the church he heard strange musical sounds, and decided to investigate where the noises were coming from. As he walked towards the sounds he encountered a beautiful apparition of the Virgin Mary.

His encounter was on Tepeyac Hill, which was the site of a former Aztec temple. The Virgin appeared to him as a native princess, and he was taken aback by her incredible beauty and her musical voice. She assured Juan of her identity, and instructed him to visit the local bishop and to tell him to build a temple on the site of her miraculous apparition.

He duly did as he was instructed but the bishop dismissed him. Filled with doubt about the apparition he returned to the site, and Mary appeared once more. She instructed him to go to the bishop and to make the request once again the following morning. Again he made the same request. But the bishop, doubting Juan, asked him to bring forward a sign from Mary. Juan said that he would return with a sign from her the next morning.

Unfortunately that evening Juan returned home to find his elderly uncle gravely ill. Unable to leave him, Juan stayed by his uncle's side for two days, tending to his fever and fearing that he would die. When it became apparent that his death was near, Juan left his uncle's side to find a priest to prepare for his passing and to hear his last confession.

Juan set off in a hurry but was halted by a third apparition of Mary. Mary chided Juan, and he felt shameful, but still he asked for a sign to give to the bishop. Mary instructed him to climb to the top of Tepeyac Hill. There he found roses that were not native to the area and could not possibly grow there naturally in the December cold. He picked the flowers and hid them in his tilma, a type of cloak.

Once more Juan went to see the bishop, who had now been waiting for two days for Juan to come with a sign from Mary. Juan went to the bishop and opened his cloak, and the roses cascaded to the floor. To their astonishment they saw that an image of Mary was imprinted on the inside of his cloak.

Simultaneously, while appearing to Juan and directing him to the flowers, Mary appeared in a vision to his uncle. His fever ended, leaving him feeling well again. She stated to Juan's uncle him that she wished to be known as Santa Maria de Guadalupe.

The exquisite image that was imprinted on Juan's cloak is displayed today in the Basilica de Guadalupe. The image is of Mary appearing as a native princess, with her head bowed and her hands folded in prayer. In the image she is depicted as wearing a blue cloak with the stars arranged on it as they were in the sky on the dusky morning of her first apparition. Under her feet sits a symbol of the old Aztec religion, a crescent moon. Underneath the moon is an angel, arms outstretched and supporting Mary as if transporting her. The angel has wings of an eagle and is called the Virgin of Guadalupe's Angel. The angel's face is of a child but it has the qualities of an older face, full of wisdom. It is believed that the original image has many supernatural and miraculous properties.

Neither the image nor the material of the tilma has degraded over time, despite being five hundred years old. Pope John Paul II canonised Juan Diego in 2002, which made him the first indigenous American saint.

Padre Pio

Padre Pio was born in Italy in May 1887 into a poor family. In 1910 he was ordained as a Catholic priest and spent most of his time in prayer. He often conversed out loud with his guardian angel as well as with Jesus, Mary and St Francis. He often suggested that if people needed spiritual help that they should send him their guardian angels and not come in person. It was said that Padre often sent his own guardian angel out to help others. He rarely left the monastery where he resided, never read a newspaper or listened to the radio, and lived in poverty with very little in the way of possessions or comforts.

In 1918 marks of stigmata appeared on his body, similar to the wounds of Christ, as he was praying in front of a crucifix after Mass. He became the first stigmatised priest in the history of the Church and bore the often painful wounds for fifty years.

His angel supposedly undertook many tasks, including translating foreign letters for him, repeatedly knocking on the door of his companion (who regularly overslept) and even allegedly chauffeured a man who went to sleep at the wheel of his car.

Padre Pio's fame spread, and when he died in 1968 almost a hundred thousand people came to his funeral. Many make the pilgrimage to his former home and his burial place to this day.

The Angels of Fátima

Three children were leading their family flock of sheep to pasture when they encountered an angel. The children were Lúcia, aged nine, Francisco, aged eight, and Jacinta, aged six. The angel of peace appeared to them three times before the appearances of Mother Mary at Fátima, Portugal. The angel taught the children to pray and told them that Mother Mary would appear to them, which she did one year later and on the thirteenth day of every month for six months. She entrusted the children with three secrets. Lúcia became a nun and continued to have visions throughout her life.

On 13 October 1917 an event known as the Miracle of the Sun occurred. A large crowd of around sixty thousand people appeared in response to the children and the prophecy that they had been given, which was that the Virgin Mary would appear and perform miracles. Witnesses claimed that the sun appeared to zigzag or dance in the sky, emitting multicoloured lights. The event lasted ten minutes. It is known as the day that the sun danced.

Fátima today is one of the most important Roman Catholic shrines in the world that is dedicated to the Virgin Mary.

John of God

João Teixeira de Faria, also known as John of God, is a famous Brazilian healer. For nearly thirty years millions of people have visited Abadiânia, a remote village in Brazil, where he carries out his healing work at the *casa*, a spiritual healing centre. He performs many psychic surgeries but states that all healing ultimately comes from God.

Born in 1942, John of God is now in his late seventies. It is said that King Solomon entered his body while still in his teens. He says that up to thirty entities can work through him to give healing and that some of these entities are long-deceased physicians, surgeons and saints. However, only one of these entities at a time will work through him.

People who visit the *casa* complex where he resides stay there for two weeks and must follow strict rules both during their stay and after, because he says the entities continue their work long after visiting the *casa*.

It is said that the location of the spiritual healing centre and *casa* complex, which is situated above a crystal cave, was picked by John of God due to its high energy.

He has performed many miraculous healings, although he professes that not everyone can be cured.

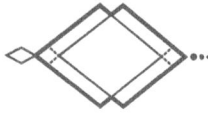

Chapter 14

Angel Quotes to Inspire

Here are a few quotes on angels for inspiration, meditation and reflection.

A good angel will accompany him; his journey will be successful, and he will come back in good health.
—Tobit 5:22

All around the throne of God a band
Of glorious Angels always stand.
—James Heale

All God's angels come to us disguised.
—James Russell Lowell

Angels and ministers of grace, defend us!
—William Shakespeare

Angels are pure thoughts from God, winged with Truth and Love.
—Mary Baker Eddy

*Angels descending, bringing from above,
Echoes of mercy, whispers of love.*
—Fanny J. Crosby

Are not all angels' spirits in the divine service, sent to serve for the sake of those who are to inherit salvation?
—Hebrews 1:14

*Around our pillows golden ladders rise,
And up and down the skies,
With winged sandals shod
The angels come and go
The Messengers of God.*
—Richard Henry Stoddard

As much of heaven is visible as we have eyes to see.
—Ralph Waldo Emerson

Be an angel to someone else whenever you can, as a way of thanking God for the help your angel has given you.
—Eileen Elias Freeman

*Beside each man who's born on Earth,
A guardian angel takes his stand,*

To guide him through life's mysteries.
—Menander of Athens

Do not neglect to show hospitality to strangers,
for by doing that some have entertained angels
without knowing it.
—Hebrews 13:2

Ever felt an angel's breath in the gentle breeze?
A teardrop in the falling rain? Hear a whisper
among the rustle of the leaves? Or been kissed by
a lone snowflake? Nature is an angel's favourite
hiding place.
—Carrie Latet

Every blade of grass has its angel that bends over
it and whispers, 'Grow, grow.'
—The Talmud

Every visible thing in this world is put in the
charge of an angel.
—Saint Augustine

For He will command His angels concerning you
to guard you in all your ways.
They will lift you up in their hands, so that you
will not strike your foot against a stone.
—Psalm 91: 11,12

*God committed the care of men and all things
under heaven to angels.*
—Justin Martyr

*I am going to send an angel in front of you, to
guard you on the way.*
—Exodus 23:20

*If I have freedom in my love,
And in my soul am free,
Angels alone that soar above,
Enjoy such liberty.*
—Richard Lovelace

*If instead of a gem, or even a flower, we should
cast the gift of a loving thought into the heart of a
friend, that would be giving as the angels give.*
—George MacDonald

*If these beings guard you, they do so because
they have been summoned by your prayers.*
—Saint Ambrose

*In this dim world of cloudy cares,
We rarely know, till wildered eyes,
See white wings lessening up the skies,
The angels with us unawares.*
—Gerald T. Massey

Make yourself familiar with the angels, and behold them frequently in spirit, for without being seen, they are present with you.
—Saint Francis de Sales

No, I never saw an angel, but it is irrelevant whether I saw them or not. I feel their presence around me.
—Paulo Coelho

One of the hardest lessons we have to learn in this life … is to see the divine, the celestial, the pure in the common, the near at hand – to see that heaven lies above us here in this world.
—John Burroughs

Pay attention to your dreams – God's angels often speak directly to our hearts when we are asleep.
—Eileen Elias Freemen

So the angel that was to come to talk with me held me, comforted me, and set me up upon my feet.
—2 Esdras 5:15

The angel said to them, 'Do not be afraid; for see, I am bringing you good news of great joy for all the people.'
—Luke 2:10

The function of the wing is to take what is heavy and raise it up in the region above.
—Plato

The greatest achievement was at first and for a time a dream. The oak sleeps in the acorn, the bird waits in the egg, and in the highest vision of the soul a waking angel stirs. Dreams are the seedlings of realities.
—James Allen

The guardian angels of life sometimes fly so high as to be beyond our sight, but they are always looking down upon us.
—Jean Paul Richter

Therefore, with angels and archangels, and with all the company of heaven, we laud and magnify thy glorious Name, evermore praising thee.
—The Book of Common Prayer

These things I warmly wish for you –
Someone to love
Some work to do
A bit o' sun
A bit o' cheer
And a guardian angel
Always near
—Old Irish Greeting

We should pray to the angels, for they are given to us as guardians.
—Saint Ambrose

Appendix 1

The Auric Egg Breathing Exercise

This is a cleansing breath exercise to purify and strengthen the aura, the energy field around the body. This can be practised first thing in the morning upon awakening to prepare you for the day ahead, or it can be done at night to get rid of any negativity or stress that you have encountered during your day. With this exercise you are the yolk inside the egg.

Between the yolk and the shell are seven other layers, the layers of the aura or the energetic field surrounding the body. This breathing exercise will help in cleansing and strengthening the aura.

On the in breath visualise that you are breathing up the back of the body from the backs of the feet to the top of the head.

On the out breath visualise the breath going down the front side of the body, sweeping under the feet.

Do this circular breathing from back to front seven times. Each time visualise that you have moved slightly away from the body in an ever-expanding circle, until on the seventh breath it is at arm's length away from the body.

Then breathe up the left side of the body from the sides of the feet up and over the head.

On the out breath breathe down the right side of the body, sweeping under the feet.

Do this circular breathing from left to right seven times. Each time visualise that you have breathed the aura slightly away from the body in an ever-expanding circle, until on the seventh breath it is at arm's length away from the body.

Visualise yourself with a cleansed auric field like the shape of an egg that surrounds the body.

If you wish you can alternate between back to front and then left to right, breathing seven times.

Appendix 2

White Light Meditation

Find a quiet place where you will not be disturbed. Sit in a comfortable position. It is better to do this meditation sitting upright rather than lying down, as the energies will travel through the top of your head and through the body. You may wish to light a candle and perhaps burn some incense.

Close your eyes. Take a deep breath. As you breathe in, imagine breathing in peace. On the out breath, breathe away all tension and anxiety. Breathe in peace and love. Breathe out all tension, stresses and strains. As you breathe in, imagine all the tensions of the day and any thoughts and fears melting away with the out breath.

Continue to breathe in and out in this way until you feel calm and relaxed. Now begin to imagine a pure crystalline or white light above your head. This white light is pure and full of love and peace.

Breathe in this white light through the top of your head. As it enters your head, feel it melt away all thoughts and fears, leaving your mind still and peaceful. Breathe out.

As you continue to gently breathe in and out, feel the white light moving down the back of your head, making your head relaxed. Feel the white light moving over your eyes and face, making all the muscles relaxed.

As you continue to breathe, feel the white light now moving down your neck, through your shoulders, making them relaxed. Now feel the light travel down your arms as it travels down your fingers and thumbs, taking all tension with it and leaving your arms feeling relaxed.

Now take this light from your shoulders down through your spine as it travels through your trunk, relaxing all the muscles and organs as it goes through your body.

Feel the light now travel down over your hips, through your thighs, knees, calves and ankles and out through your heels, leaving your whole body calm, relaxed and at peace.

Feel roots now, growing from the soles of your feet, down into the earth, anchoring and grounding you. Feel these roots grow and expand deep into the earth, like the roots of an oak tree, firm and strong. As these roots go deep into the earth they find a crystal and the roots wrap themselves around this crystal.

Now draw the pure energy from the crystal back up through the soles of your feet, through your ankles, calves, knees and hips.

Feel the energy from the crystal move up through

your trunk, stomach, chest and internal organs as it travels up your spine to the base of your head. Take the energy of the crystal across your shoulders and down through your fingers and thumbs.

Now feel the crystal energy move up through your head as it moves to your crown. Feel this energy flow out through the top of your head as it now begins to flow outwards, filling your energy field with pure, crystalline energy. Feel it filling and expanding through your energy field at arm's length all around your body.

Sit in this energy feeling peaceful, relaxed and healthy for a few minutes. If your mind wanders at all, focus on the gentle rise and fall of your breath.

Now begin to bring yourself back. Feel the streaming of the white light disconnect. Feel yourself sitting in the chair. Move your fingers and toes and feel aware of your surroundings.

When you feel ready, seal and protect this wonderful energy within your own energy field. Clench your fists and imagine a sphere of protection fifteen feet below you, above you, in front of you, behind you and at both sides, all around you like a huge translucent bubble protecting you and keeping you safe. To finish, if you can, reach down and put your palms on the top of your feet to ground yourself. If you can't reach that far just run your palms down your legs as far as they will go. Stay there for a few seconds, then sit up and open your eyes.

Appendix 3

The Chakra Meditation

Find a quiet place to sit where you will not be disturbed. Turn off the phone. If you wish you can light a candle, burn some incense or put on some soft music. Do whatever makes you feel happy.

Sit with your feet flat on the ground. Close your eyes. Take a few slow, deep breaths. As you do this, start to connect with the universal white light of the divine consciousness. Breathe in this white light as you have done before in the white light meditation.

Visualise a shaft of pure crystalline light coming down from the cosmos and entering the top of your head. See it engulfing your body inside and out, leaving through the soles of your feet, cleansing all negative energies as it travels through your body.

When you have breathed in the white light, concentrate on the soles of your feet. See roots like those of a tree sink deep into the earth, grounding you.

See the energy of the earth move up your body as it

reaches your base chakra situated in your perineum. Breathe in the colour red. As you breathe in the colour red see your chakra become balanced with a red hue. If you see any muddiness or imbalance, breathe it away.

When you are ready, take the energy up to the sacral chakra situated below your belly button. Breathe in the colour orange. As you breathe in the colour orange see your chakra become balanced with an orange hue. If you see any muddiness or imbalance, breathe it away.

When you are ready take the energy up to the solar plexus chakra situated above your belly button and below your chest. Breathe in golden yellow. As you breathe in the colour yellow see your chakra become balanced with a yellow hue. If you see any muddiness or imbalance, breathe it away.

When you are ready take the energy up to the heart chakra situated in the chest. Visualise it in a bright green and see it expanding in loving radiance. As you breathe in the colour green see your chakra become balanced with a green hue. If you see any muddiness or imbalance, breathe it away.

Next take the energy up to the throat chakra situated in the throat. Breathe in the colour blue, a bright blue. As you breathe in the colour blue see your chakra become balanced with a blue hue. If you see any muddiness or imbalance, breathe it away.

Now take the energy up to the third eye chakra situated on the bridge of your nose. Breathe in the colour indigo. As you breathe in the colour indigo see your chakra become balanced with an indigo hue. If you see any muddiness or imbalance, breathe it away.

Move your attention now to the top of your head, where the crown chakra is situated. Breathe in the colour violet. As you breathe in the colour violet see your chakra become balanced with a violet hue. If you see any muddiness or imbalance, breathe it away.

Now sit for a few moments as you feel all your chakras balanced and aligned.

When you are ready to finish, breathe each chakra back in turn, still retaining its assigned colour.

Start with the crown chakra. Breathe and see it return to its normal size, balanced and aligned.

Then move to the third eye chakra. Breathe and see it return to its normal size, balanced and aligned.

Then move to the throat chakra. Breathe and see it return to its normal size, balanced and aligned.

Then move to the heart chakra. Breathe and see it return to its normal size, balanced and aligned.

Then move to the solar plexus chakra. Breathe and see it return to its normal size, balanced and aligned.

Then move to the sacral chakra. Breathe and see it return to its normal size, balanced and aligned.

Then finally move to the base chakra. Breathe and see it return to its normal size, balanced and aligned.

Feel your whole body healthy, balanced, aligned and refreshed. Open your eyes when you are ready. Stretch and touch your feet to ground yourself.

Appendix 4

Chakra Energy Centre Meditation

Sit with your feet and arms uncrossed, with your feet firmly connected to the floor (you may wish to put a cushion or something similar under the feet so that they are connected to the floor).

Close your eyes. Take a few long, slow, deep breaths. Be still.

Now see a pure crystalline light descend from the cosmos until it settles just above your head. It is a light of pure radiance, peace and tranquillity. It is light and it is love.

Feel the peace descend all around you and illuminating radiance from within. You are a divine light, a spark of that divine radiance.

Begin to breathe in the white light now.

Breathe in the white light through the top of your head as it takes away all your cares and worries, stilling the mind. See all your troubles and thoughts just melt away. Be of peace. You connect with the wisdom of the divine, higher knowledge and guidance.

Take the white light now down into your third eye, just above the bridge of your nose between the eyebrows. It gives you clear inner vision of mind, of body and of soul. You see with clarity of vision, physically and through your mind's eye.

Now take the white light into the throat area. If the need arises, clear your throat and do so without hesitation.

Here the white light clears the throat area for clear communication, creativity and listening.

See the white light now move into the heart area. See this area expand with a deep sense of love and compassion – love for yourself and for all beings. Feel and sense the love expanding with radiance.

Move the white light now to the solar plexus area, the centre of the body, just below the ribcage. See the white light remove anxiety, worry and stress. Feel yourself centred, calm and empowered.

Next move the white light to the sacral centre, just above the pubis. See the white light clear away any feelings of guilt or shame. Feel the light connect with procreation, sexuality and creativity.

Next move the white light to the base, the perineum, the seat on which you sit. Feel the white light remove any insecurities or worries about the future. It gives stability and strength, setting firm foundations.

Now see the white light travel down the legs through the soles of the feet and into the earth as if you have roots, like the roots of trees coming from the feet, anchoring you firmly to the earth. See the white light taking away all negative energies, away from your body and into the earth to be transmuted into positive energy.

Now take a breath and breathe the light in a circular motion from the feet, up the back of the body and down over the front of the body. Breathe it down into the feet. Breathe in this circular motion up the rear of the body and down the front three times.

Now breathe the white light up the left side of the body from the feet to the top of the head, and down the right side of the body to the feet. Breathe in this circular motion up the left and down the right side of the body three times.

Now we are going to stay here for a minute or maybe longer, enjoying the peaceful energies.

Wait for at least a minute to elapse.

Now it is time to come back into full alertness and awake on the count of three.

One… Coming back to full alertness.

Two… Feeling happy, peaceful and relaxed.

Three… Open your eyes, fully awake and alert.

Stretch and touch your feet if you can.

Record any experiences in your journal.

Appendix 5

Connecting with Your Guardian Angel in Meditation

Everyone has a guardian angel watching over them. This angel gives protection and guidance and assists in the development and evolution of the soul, possibly through many lifetimes. Communication and connection with your guardian angel can be very helpful in all healing work and in developing the spiritual path. This is a simple way in which to contact your guardian angel.

Sit in a quiet place where you will not be disturbed. You may wish to burn some incense and possibly a candle.

Sit with the intention that you are to connect with your guardian angel. Visualise a light presence behind and just above you. This is the light presence emanating from your guardian angel. Visualise your guardian angel stepping into your aura and merging with you, and feel your guardian angel's presence both within and around you. Feel the divine, loving embrace of your angel. Feel your mind and heart connect fully with your guardian angel and allow your angel to reveal itself to you fully.

When you feel that the connection has been made, sit and experience the divine love and peace that this angel has for you. You may request their help in developing your spiritual path or anything else that you feel your angel may be able to assist with.

When your communication with this angelic being is complete, give thanks for this time you have spent with them and thanks for the knowledge and love that they have imparted. Bid farewell to your guardian angel, knowing that their presence is forever around you and that you can communicate with them at any time.

This meditation can also be used to work with the presence of any archangel. Sit in meditation and follow the steps above while quietly repeating the name of the angel that you wish to work with until you feel their loving presence.

Appendix 6

Meet Your Guardian Angel Visualisation

Find a place where you will not be disturbed. Switch off any phones. You may wish to light a candle or burn some incense. Sit comfortably in a chair with your feet flat on the floor and your hands resting in your lap.

Close your eyes. Take a deep breath. As you breathe in, imagine breathing in peace. On the out breath, breathe away all tension and anxiety. Breathe in peace and love. Breathe out all tension, stresses and strains. As you breathe, imagine all the tensions of the day and any thoughts and fears melting away with the out breath.

Focus on the soles of your feet. Imagine roots like the roots of trees coming out through the soles of the feet, travelling deep, deep down into the earth, grounding you. Focus once more on the breath.

See yourself walking down a garden path. You feel the warmth of the sun on your face and a slight breeze in the air. Attached to a belt around your waist is a small pouch that you can use to collect any objects you gather on your journey.

As you walk down the path you see a gate in front of you set in a wall. This is the entrance to a walled garden. You open the gate and enter the garden. You close the gate behind you. In front of you is a bench on which to sit. You sit down on the bench for a few moments as you look around the garden.

Take a few moments here to rest.

When you are ready you look down and see that there is a magic carpet by your feet. You sit down on the magic carpet and it lifts off the ground. You feel stable and safe.

The magic carpet lifts upwards towards the clouds above. The garden below gets further and further away as you go higher. You are not frightened and feel safe.

You break through the clouds. There, hidden above the clouds, is a magical place. It is the realm of the angelic beings. Everything is white, bright and beautiful. The magic carpet settles gently down and you step off the carpet to explore this wondrous place. You hear soft harp music playing in the background. There is a central fountain running with pure, crystalline healing waters. There are seats around the water fountain.

You see in front of you a group of angelic beings dressed in robes. The group parts as a familiar being walks towards you. You recognise this being immediately. It is your guardian angel. You look into their beautiful face and look deep into their eyes. You look carefully at their features so that you will instantly recognise them again.

You both sit together by the fountain. You ask your guardian angel for a name so that you can call them when needed. You take a few moments to listen carefully.

You both look into the pool of water. You ask your guardian angel to show you your life's purpose. You watch together as your guardian angel shows you images that are reflected in the water. Perhaps your guardian angel has other information they wish you to know.

You stay there for a few moments, watching and listening.

Sadly, it is now time for you to go. Your guardian angel takes you in a loving embrace. As you part your guardian angel gives you a gift. You look at the gift and put it in your pouch for safekeeping. You walk back to your magic carpet, ready to go home, but you know that you can return there anytime you want to. You step on the magic carpet and it lifts up slightly. You give a wave to your guardian angel.

The magic carpet makes its way back down through the clouds. You see the garden below getting nearer and nearer. You land safely, back to where you set off. You step off the carpet. You take one last look around the garden.

You give thanks for your wonderful experience. You walk towards the gate set in the wall. You open the gate, walk through it and close the gate behind you. You walk back down the path. You still have the gift in your pouch.

You now become aware of the room you are sitting in and feel the chair you are sitting on. You feel yourself aware, sitting, back where you started. Full awareness is coming back now.

Open your eyes when you are ready. Take a full stretch.

Write your experiences in your journal while you remember them.

Appendix 7

Calling in the Archangels of the Quarters (the Cardinal Winds)

The archangels can be asked to oversee and protect any energetic working, whether it is healing work, prayer, meditation or any ritual. Normally this exercise is used with just the first four archangels. A variation on this, though, is to have Metatron above and Sandalphon below. This is down to personal preference. Do what feels right for you.

To begin, you can either sit in meditation or stand in the centre of the area where you will be working and turn to face each of the directions in turn. You may wish to burn some incense and also light a candle if desired.

Facing east, request the presence of Raphael to enter the circle with the power of healing and illumination.

Facing west, request the presence of Gabriel to enter the circle with the power of strength and divine vision.

Facing south, request the presence of Michael

to enter the circle with the power of goodness and righteousness.

Facing north, request the presence of Uriel to enter the circle with the power of divine knowledge and revelation.

In addition, if wished:

Gazing upwards with raised hands, request the presence of Archangel Metatron with the power of mercy and grace.

Gazing down and gesturing to the earth, request the presence of Archangel Sandalphon with the power of prayer and redemption.

When the presence of the archangels has been requested the act of meditation, prayer, healing or ritual can take place. You are safe in knowing that the archangels will provide guidance and protection in their holy emanations of light.

When the work is done, give thanks for the presence of the holy angels. Send each angel back in turn with a grateful and loving heart.

Appendix 8

Body of Light Merkabah Meditation

This is a wonderful meditation for self-healing and clearing. I have used this for many years, and it can be completed when needed. It can be done in a few moments or in many minutes. Time doesn't matter.

A Merkabah is an eight-pointed three-dimensional star, rather like two pyramids combined, with one pointing down and one pointing up. Don't get too bogged down with symbolism if you struggle to envisage it. You can always just visualise a bright star. If you feel that the energy is stuck or hindered in any way, stick with it until the energy travels freely through the body.

Find a place where you will not be disturbed. Switch off any phones. You may wish to light a candle or burn some incense. Sit comfortably in a chair with your feet flat on the floor and your hands resting in your lap.

Close your eyes. Take a deep breath. As you breathe in, imagine breathing in peace. On the out breath, breathe away all tension and anxiety. Breathe in peace and love. Breathe out all tension, stresses and strains. As you breathe, imagine all the tensions of the day and any thoughts melting away with the out breath.

Take your attention to the top of your head. See a small star situated at the top of your head. Visualise the star moving about six inches above the head, a hand's distance away from the top of the head.

See the star as expanding. You see that it is a Merkabah. This Merkabah is expanding slightly, glowing with a pure shining radiance.

Sense now a pure, crystalline light streaming down from the Merkabah as it enters the top of your head. The light enters your body, clearing it of all negative energies, healing and clearing as it travels through your body.

Feel it clear though the top of your head, down behind the bridge of the nose, down through the throat area. It travels down the arms and fingers, clearing as it goes. The crystalline light travels through the trunk of your body, through the solar plexus area, down through the stomach down to the base and into your hips. It travels through both of your legs, clearing and healing as it goes.

The crystalline energy now reaches your feet. Feel the crystalline energy go through the soles of your feet, removing all negative energies from your body into the earth. This energy is going out through the soles of your feet, and any negative energies are to be transmuted into positive crystalline energies by the earth.

Carry on sensing the crystalline energy travelling

through your body out of the soles of your feet until you feel that the energy is travelling through your body without restriction and that the body feels clear and full of radiant, divine, crystalline light from your Merkabah. This may take a few minutes.

When you are ready, see the soles of the feet 'close' so that the crystalline light is no longer coming out of the body. Now the crystalline light builds a light body within your own body. Your whole body is filling with crystalline light from the feet upwards until the body is so full of light energy that it begins to come out of the top of your head like a fountain of radiant light. See the light now fill up your aura, like an egg of light surrounding your body at arm's length all around.

When you feel ready, it is now time to switch off the Merkabah. The crystalline light comes to a slow halt as its job is done. Visualise the Merkabah now, reducing back to a small star as it lowers to just above your head, back in its normal place.

Sit for a short while enjoying the feel of your body full of pure, crystalline light.

Take a few deep breaths and come around when you are ready. Take a stretch and touch your toes to ground yourself.

Appendix 9

The Prayer of Saint Francis

This is a lovely prayer accredited to Saint Francis of Assisi. However, it is believed to be French in origin and although it is not by Saint Francis it is in the spirit of his wisdom and his other wonderful prayers. It is an uplifting prayer that can be said at times when you are looking to instil some peace and serenity into your life.

Lord, make me an instrument of Your peace;
Where there is hatred, let me sow love;
Where there is injury, pardon;
Where there is doubt, faith;
Where there is despair, hope;
Where there is darkness, light;
And where there is sadness, joy.

O Divine Master,
Grant that I may not so much seek
To be consoled as to console;

To be understood, as to understand;
To be loved, as to love;
For it is in giving that we receive,
It is in pardoning that we are pardoned,
And it is in dying that we are born to Eternal Life.
Amen.

Biblical References

The angels are mentioned many times in biblical texts. Here are some references that have either been mentioned in the text or are references to angels that you may wish to look up. These references do not include any from the book Ezekiel, which is worthy of study on its own.

Genesis	3:24	16:7, 9—11	19:1, 15
	21:17	22:11, 15	24:7, 40
	28:12	31:11	32:1
	48:16		
Exodus	3:2	14:19	23:20, 23
	32:34	33:2	
Numbers	20:16	22:22–27, 31, 32, 34, 35	
Deuteronomy	33:2		
Judges	2:1, 4	5:23	6:11, 12, 20—22
	13:3, 6, 9, 13, 15—21		
1 Samuel	29:9		
2 Samuel	14:17, 20	19:27	24:16, 17
1 Kings	13:18	19:5, 7	

2 Kings	1:3, 15	19:35	
1 Chronicles	21:12, 15, 16, 18, 20, 27, 30		
2 Chronicles	32:21		
Job	4:18		
Psalms	8:5	34:7	35:5, 6
	68:17	78:25, 49	91:1, 11, 12
	103:20	104:4	148:2
Ecclesiastes	5:6		
Isaiah	6:1–7	37:36	63:9
Daniel	3:28	6:22	8:16
	9:21	10:3, 6, 21	12:1
Hosea	12:4		
Zechariah	1:9, 11—14, 19	2:3	3:1, 3, 5, 6
	4:1, 4, 5	5:5, 10	6:4, 5
	12:8		
Matthew	1:20, 24	2:13, 19	4:6, 11
	13:39, 41, 49	16:27	18:10
	22:30	24:31, 36	25:31, 41
	26:53	28:2, 5	
Mark	1:13	8:38	12:25
	13:27, 32		

Luke	1:5, 11, 13, 18, 19, 26, 28, 30, 34, 35, 38	2:9, 10, 13, 15, 21	4:10
	9:26	12:8, 9	15:8—10
	16:22	20:36	22:43
	24:23		
John	1:51	5:2—4	12:29
	20:12		
Acts	5:19	6:15	7:30, 35, 38, 53
	8:26	10:3, 7, 22	11:13
	12:7—11, 15, 23	23:8, 9	27:23
Romans	8:38		
1 Corinthians	4:9	6:3	
2 Corinthians	11:14		
Galatians	1:8	3:19	4:14
Colossians	1:16	2:18	
1 Thessalonians	4:16		
2 Thessalonians	1:7		
1 Timothy	3:16	5:21	
Hebrews	1:4—7, 13, 14	2:2, 5, 7, 9, 16	12:22
	13:2		

191

1 Peter	1:12	3:22	
2 Peter	2:4, 11		
Jude	1:6, 9		
Revelation	1:1, 20	2:1, 8, 12, 18	3:1, 5, 7, 14
	4:1—11	5:2, 11, 12	7:1, 2, 11
	8:2—8, 10, 12, 13	9:1, 11, 13—15	10:1, 5, 7—10
	11:1, 15	12:7, 9	14:6, 8—10, 15, 17—19
	15:1, 6—8	16:1, 3—5, 8, 10, 12, 17	17:1, 7
	18:1, 21	19:17	20:1
	21:9, 12, 17	22:6, 8, 16	

APOCRYPHA SOURCES

2 Esdras	1:19, 40	2:44, 46, 48	4:1, 36
	5:15, 20, 31	6:3	7:1
	8:21	10:28	12:51
	16:66		
Tobit	3:25 8:3, 15	5:4, 6, 16, 21, 22	6:3–6, 10, 13, 15
	11:14	12:5, 15, 22	
Additions to Esther	15:13		
Wisdom of Solomon	16:20		

Ecclesiasticus	48:21	
Letter to Jeremiah	1:7	
Prayer of Azariah	1:26, 37	
Susanna	1:59	
Bel and the Dragon	1:34, 36, 39	
1 Maccabees	7:41	
2 Maccabees	11:6	15:22, 23

References and Further Reading

Andrews, T., *How to Meet and Work with Spirit Guides*, (1992), Llewellyn Publications, Minnesota, USA.

Cooper, D., *Angel Inspiration: How to Change Your World with the Angels*, (2004), Hodder & Stoughton, London.

Davidson, G., *A Dictionary of Angels Including the Fallen Angels*, (1994), Free Press (a division of Macmillan), New York.

Dyer, W., Dr, *The Power of Intention*, (2010), Hay House, USA.

Editors of Beliefnet, *The Big Book of Angels*, (2003), Hinkler Books Pty Ltd, Australia.

Gallery, J., *And God Created Angels,* (2001), Brighton Books, Nashville, TN, USA.

Graham, B., *Angels*, (1994), Word Publishing, USA.

Hall, J, *The Crystal Bible: Volume 1*, (2009), Godsfield Press, Division of Octopus Publishing Group, London.

Howarth Tomlinson, T., *Walking into the Light: A Seeker's Guide to Spiritual Development*, (2018), 2QT, UK.

Keck, D., *Angels and Angelology in the Middle Ages*, (1998), Oxford University Press, New York.

Malachi, T., Houston, S., *Gnostic Healing: Revealing the Hidden Power of God*, (2010), Llewellyn Publications, Minnesota, USA.

Malachi, T., *Gnosis of the Cosmic Christ: A Gnostic Christian Kabbalah*, (2011), Llewellyn Publications, Minnesota, USA.

Nyland, A., Dr, *Angels, Archangels and Angel Categories: What the Ancients Said*, (2010), Smith and Sterling, Queensland, Australia.

Pope John Paul II, *The Catechism of the Catholic Church*, (2000), Bantam Doubleday Bell, USA (first published 1992).

Ronner, J. E., K*now Your Angels: The Angel Almanac With Biographies of 100 Prominent Angels in Legend & Folklore – and Much More!*, (1993),

Mamre Press, Tennessee, USA.

Siddhanath, Y. G., Babaji: *The Lightning Standing Still*, (2012), Hamsa Yoga Sangh, Alamo, California, USA.

Smedley, J., *Angel Whispers: How to Get Closer to Your Angels*, (2009), Hay House UK Ltd, London.

Virtue, D., *The Angel Therapy Handbook*, (2011), Hay House UK Ltd, London.

Virtue D., *Archangels and Ascended Masters*, (2009), Hay House UK Ltd, London.

Virtue, D., *Healing with the Angels: How the Angels Can Assist You in Every Area of Your Life*, (2006), Hay House UK Ltd, London.

Virtue, D., *How to Hear Your Angels*, (2007), Hay House UK Ltd, London.

Virtue, D., *The Lightworker's Way: Awakening Your Spiritual Power to Know and Heal*, (2010), Hay House UK Ltd, London.

Yogananda, P., *Autobiography of a Yogi*, (2015 reprint of the 1946 original), Crystal Clarity Publishers, USA.

9 781912 014316